This book is due for return on or before the last date shown below.

GREENWICH EXCHANGE
LONDON

Greenwich Exchange, London

First published in Great Britain in 2006
All rights reserved

Lord Byron © Andrew Keanie 2006

Printed and bound by Q3 Digital/Litho, Loughborough
Tel: 01509 213456
Typesetting and layout by Albion Associates, London
Tel: 020 8852 4646
Cover design by December Publications, Belfast
Tel: 028 90286559

Cover picture: Mary Evans Picture Library

Greenwich Exchange Website: www.greenex.co.uk

ISBN-13: 978-1-871551-83-9
ISBN-10: 1-871551-83-8

to Mum

Byron! how sweetly sad thy melody!
Attuning still the soul to tenderness,
As if soft Pity, with unusual stress,
Had touch'd her plaintive lute, and thou, being by,
Hadst caught the tones, nor suffer'd them to die.
O'ershadowing sorrow doth not make thee less
Delightful: thou thy griefs dost dress
With a bright halo, shining beamily,
As when a cloud the golden moon doth veil,
Its sides are ting'd with a resplendent glow,
Through the dark robe oft amber rays prevail,
And like fair veins in sable marble flow;
Still warble, dying swan! still tell the tale,
The enchanting tale, the tale of pleasing woe.

John Keats, 'Sonnet to Byron'

No one has questioned his supremacy as a satirist. Perhaps the originality both of his wit and humour is not sufficiently recognised … He is the parent of modern fun.

Ernest Hartley Coleridge

Contents

Chronology

1788   Born 22nd January, London.

1789   Mother takes him to Aberdeen.

1791   Father, Captain John ('Mad Jack') Byron, dies.

1793   Goes to grammar school in Aberdeen.

1798   5th Lord Byron ("the wicked Lord"), Byron's great uncle, dies. Byron becomes 6th Baron Byron of Rochdale.

1801   Goes to Harrow School.

1805   Goes to Trinity College, Cambridge.

1806   *Fugitive Pieces* privately printed.

1807   *Poems on Various Occasions* privately printed. *Hours of Idleness* published. Becomes friend of John Cam Hobhouse.

1808   *Hours of Idleness* is reviewed unfavourably.

1809   *English Bards and Scotch Reviewers* published. Albania, Greece, Turkey, and Asia Minor included in Byron's Grand Tour.

1811   Returns to England. Mother dies. The Trinity Chorister, John Edleston (with whom Byron had a love-affair), dies.

1812   *Childe Harold's Pilgrimage*, Cantos I and II, published. Meets Anabella Milbanke.

1813   *The Giaour* published. Love affair with Augusta Leigh.

1814   *The Corsair* published. Proposes to Anabella.

1815   Marries Annabella. *Hebrew Melodies* published. Byron's daughter, Augusta Ada, born.

1816   Exile in Italy. Meets Percy Bysshe Shelley.

1817   *Manfred* published. Daughter, Allegra born to Claire Clairmont (Shelley's sister).

1818   *Beppo* published. *Childe Harold*, Canto IV, published.

1819   *Don Juan*, Cantos I and II published.

1821   *Don Juan*, Cantos III-V, published.

1822   *The Vision of Judgment* published.

1823   *Don Juan*, Cantos VI-XIV published. Sails for Greece.

1824   Dies at Missolonghi, 30th December.

1

Byron and his times

The convulsion known as the Romantic Movement was urged by many longings in millions of minds, some, perhaps, only eager to destroy existing authorities, many hungry for freedom to use the inventive faculties special to each human soul, and many others hungering and thirsting for the mystical experiences of religion. The results of these longings may be seen in the French Revolution and its sequent wars ... All these hungers of mind affected poetry, which is itself often a hunger of the mind.

John Masefield, first published in 1946 by
William Heinemann Ltd

The poetic revolution of William Wordsworth (1770-1850) and Samuel Taylor Coleridge (1772-1834) – one thinks of their joint *Lyrical Ballads* collection of 1798 – was the driving force behind the new thinking. By the end of the Napoleonic wars, during 1812-1815 – when England was about to cease hostilities with France – the poetic revolution of Wordsworth and Coleridge was about to stall. Wordsworth got a job as a tax collector and Coleridge was writing editorials for right-wing newspapers, and the other Lake poet, Robert Southey (1774-1843), became Poet Laureate (1813-43), writing sycophantic poems about the King and the Prince of Wales. For the younger poets, that was a failure of courage. Wordsworth paid a high price for it in terms of imagination. Geoffrey Hartman is among the many admirers of Wordsworth's contributions to the *Lyrical Ballads* who has found his long poem, *The Excursion* (1814), "massively depressing" (*Wordsworth's Poetry*, 292). Lord Byron (1788-1824) would make it clear in the Preface to his satirical poem, *The Vision of Judgment* (written in 1821), that he was responding directly to

Southey's latest absurdly career-minded utterance, *A Vision of Judgment* (1821):

> If there is anything obnoxious to the political opinions of a portion of the public in the following poem, they may thank Mr Southey. He might have written hexameters, as he has written everything else, for ought that the writer cared – had they been upon another subject. But to attempt to canonise a monarch, who, whatever were his household virtues, was neither a successful nor a patriot king, – inasmuch as several years of his reign passed in war with America and Ireland, to say nothing of the aggression upon France, – like all other exaggeration, necessarily begets opposition. In whatever manner he may be spoken of in this new 'Vision', his *public* career will not be more favourably transmitted by history. Of his private virtues (although a little expensive to the nation) there can be no doubt.

Similarly, the essayist William Hazlitt (1778-1830), staunchly republican all his life, was disillusioned with the older poets' transparently self-interested transmogrifications. However, the group of poets now known as the second-generation Romantics – Byron, John Keats (1795-1821) and Percy Bysshe Shelley (1792-1822) – arrived. The categorisations – second-generation Romantics (Byron, Keats and Shelley) and first-generation Romantics (Wordsworth and Coleridge) – were not used at the time, but were later terms that would come from 20th-century literary history. The term used at the time for the group associated with the editor, poet and publisher, Leigh Hunt (1784-1859), in which Hazlitt participated and for which Keats was the leading poet, was the 'Cockney' school, which is a condescending term used by well-to-do, well-established literary reviewers; on the other hand, Byron and Shelley were associated with the so-called 'Satanic' school, again, a term of condemnation bound up with the poets' atheism and their questioning of traditional religion. Hence, Byron and Shelley are in one group, and Keats is in another, but in terms of their poetic styles, there are various and numerous overlaps, not least because all three poets use very elaborate forms of poetic language, rich with metaphor, but also full of classical allusions. The similarities of style can be seen clearly enough from a 20th-century literary historian's perspective, but at the time the

'Cockney' and 'Satanic' were perceived as two totally different categories.

After the Battle of Waterloo (1815), one of the things that drove the new generation of poets forward was the sense that Wordsworth and Coleridge had somehow gone astray, and that something new was needed. Byron, Keats and Shelley (all born in the early 1790s) were children of the Revolution, and in a sense children of Wordsworth and Coleridge (both born in the early 1770s). The model of Wordsworth and Coleridge as poetic revolutionaries was extremely powerful to them. Hazlitt's essay, 'My First Acquaintance With Poets' (1822), all about Hazlitt's first meetings with Wordsworth and Coleridge in 1798, conveys a sense of a whole new beginning for English literature, and therefore possibly for English society as well. In that essay, Hazlitt said of Wordsworth that: "There was ... a fire in his eye (as if he saw something in objects more than the outward appearance)", and of Coleridge that: "the light of his genius shone into my soul". Poetry mattered then more than it does now in that poets wrote with a view to improving, and eventually perfecting, their readers. The younger poets wanted to find a fresh way forward. In 'The Revolt of Islam' (1818), Shelley recalls how it felt to be shaken right through by the recognition of his calling in life – to oppose, and, eventually, to completely transform, society in Europe:

> I do remember well the hour which burst
> My spirit's sleep: a fresh May-dawn it was,
> When I walked forth upon the glittering grass,
> And wept, I knew not why: until there rose
> From the near school-room, voices, that, alas!
> Were but one echo from a world of woes –
> The harsh and grating strife of tyrants and of foes.
>
> And then I clasped my hands, and looked around,
> But none was near to mock my streaming eyes,
> Which poured their warm drops on the sunny ground –
> So without shame, I spake: – "I will be wise,
> And just, and free, and mild, if in me lies
> Such power; for I grow weary to behold
> The selfish and the strong still tyrannise
> Without reproach or check." I then controlled
> My tears, my heart grew calm ...

In one way their cosmopolitanism, in comparison with the first-generation Romantics, made finding a fresh way forward seem possible. Whereas the first-generation Romantics were becoming middle-aged, and therefore considering in earnest the benefits of Britain's often blinkered approach to the world's challenges, the second-generation Romantics were starting to think about the Orient, and broader European traditions of literature. Byron became the most exuberant expression of the latter impulse:

> The Isles of Greece, the Isles of Greece!
> Where burning Sappho loved and sung,
> Where grew the arts of War and Peace,
> Where Delos rose, and Phœbus sprung!
> Eternal summer gilds them yet,
> But all, except their Sun, is set.
>
> (*Don Juan*, III, 86 [1])

2

Byron: man and artist, as hero

"I know nought. Nothing I deny,/Admit, reject, contemn …," says Lord Byron in *Don Juan* (XIV, 3), defining his agnosticism. For Byron, until he learns more about what life (and death) means (if it means anything), he must provisionally understand that life is a squalid prison house from which there is no escape. Anyone who denies the inescapability of that provisional understanding – like Keats, whom Byron accused of "drivelling idiotism" and "mental masturbation", or Wordsworth, whose poetry Byron called "unintelligible", or Coleridge, whom Byron facetiously called upon to "explain his Explanation" of metaphysics – is a deluded fool: "we die, you know – and then–/What then? – I do not know, no more do you –" (*Don Juan*, I, 133-134).

The Byronic hero is, according to the essayist and statesman, Lord Macaulay (1800-1859):

> a man proud, moody, cynical, with defiance on his brow, and misery in his heart, a scorner of his kind, implacable in revenge, yet capable of deep and strong affection.
>
> (quoted by Christiansen, 201)

The surface of Byron's mentality is scarcely scratched by Macaulay's observation. Hazlitt's definition of poetry as "an aristocratical … faculty" (in his essay on *Coriolanus*) is useful, because it seems as if Byron is the subject, though he is not mentioned:

> [Poetry] aims at effect, it exists by contrast. It admits of no medium. It is everything by excess. It rises above the ordinary

standard of sufferings and crimes. It presents a dazzling appearance. It shows its head turretted, crowned, and crested.

There are two modes of Byronic heroism. One finds expression in the narrator – from Canto IV onwards, the "I" – of *Childe Harold's Pilgrimage* who, when his:

> Soul wanders ... demand[s] it back
> To meditate amongst decay, and stand
> A ruin amidst ruins; there to track
> Fall'n states and buried greatness, o'er a land
> Which *was* the mightiest in its old command,
> And *is* the loveliest ...
>
> (IV, 25)

The narrator of *Childe Harold* is the Hamlet figure, around whose soul sorrow has contracted. That incarnation of Byron – young, pure, noble, beautiful – is shut away from cheerful light and wholesome air, obliged to contemplate his own sinking under a load which he can neither support nor resolve to abandon:

> Existence may be borne, and the deep root
> Of life and sufferance make its firm abode
> In bare and desolated bosoms: mute
> The camel labours with the heaviest load,
> And the wolf dies in silence ...
>
> (IV, 21)

Caught up in, and insulated by, his general sense of his own apathy and fatalism, he feels nevertheless frequently compelled to perceive his life as some sort of chamber in which he is subjected to ever more ingenious tortures:

> But ever and anon of griefs subdued
> There comes a token like a Scorpion's sting,
> Scarce seen, but with fresh bitterness imbued;
> And slight withal may be the things which bring
> Back on the heart the weight which it would fling
> Aside for ever ...
>
> (IV, 23)

Like Hamlet, with his inextricably mixed feelings about "the thousand natural shocks" he inherits as a human being, Byron's soliloquist is a sort of advanced young sensualist who has already learned that pleasure is nothing if it is not pain refined, and vice versa:

> ... it may be a sound –
> A tone of music – summer's eve – or spring –
> A flower – the wind – the Ocean – which shall wound,
> Striking the electric chain wherewith we are darkly bound
> (IV, 23)

The other mode of Byronic heroism finds expression in Byron the satirist who, between high-society parties, deigns to take the measure of the elegant and hypocritical society around him, and verbally carpet-bombs it. In the following example he explodes, almost in passing, the idea that there could be such a thing as a seemingly, *and* really, happily-married couple:

> Don José and the Donna Inez led
> For some time an unhappy sort of life,
> Wishing each other, not divorced, but dead;
> They lived respectably as man and wife,
> Their conduct was exceedingly well-bred,
> And gave no outward signs of inward strife ...
> (*Don Juan*, I, 26)

It is no wonder, then, that Jane Stabler has suggested that Byron threatens to disclose "each reader as a potential hypocrite" (*Byron, Poetics and History*, 113). Byron seems to have learned from the poet, Matthew Prior (1664-1721), how to design a "conversational individualism ... to appeal to a fickle, ambitious class of purchasers" (*Byron, Poetics and History*, 59):

> On his death-bed poor Lubin lies:
> His spouse is in despair;
> With frequent sobs and mutual cries,
> They both express their care.
>
> A different cause, says parson Sly,
> The same effect may give:

Poor Lubin fears that he shall die;
His wife, that he may live.
　　　　　(Matthew Prior, 'A Reasonable Affliction', 1718)

Hilarious, and almost as if bathed in cheerful Mediterranean daylight as *Don Juan* is, the poem's roots are lost in the same Byronic darkness that nourishes the moodier *Childe Harold's Pilgrimage*:

Ecclesiastes said, "that all is vanity" –
Most modern preachers say the same, or show it
By their examples of true Christianity:
In short, all know, or very soon may know it;
And in this scene of all-confessed inanity,
By Saint, by Sage, by Preacher, and by Poet,
Must I restrain me, through the fear of strife,
From holding up the nothingness of Life?
　　　　　　　　　　　　　(*Don Juan*, VII, 6)

That darkness in Byron cannot really be fathomed. But, as Byron had his character, Manfred, say on his behalf:

My pang shall find a voice. From my youth upwards
My Spirit walked not with the souls of men,
Nor looked upon the earth with human eyes;
The thirst of their ambition was not mine,
The aim of their existence was not mine;
My joys – my griefs – my passions – and my powers,
Made me a stranger; though I wore the form,
I had no sympathy with breathing flesh ...
　　　　　　(*Manfred*, Act II, Scene 2, lines 50-57)

The German philosopher, Arthur Schopenhauer (1788-1860), an admirer of Byron, appreciated his alchemising touch. With the poet specifically in mind, Schopenhauer would write:

On hearing of the interesting events which have happened in the course of a man's experience, many people will wish that similar things had happened in their lives too, completely forgetting that they should be envious rather of the mental aptitude which lent those events the significance they possess when he describes them ... Byron's poems ... are obviously

founded upon actual facts; where it is open to a foolish reader
to envy the poet because so many delightful things happened
to him, instead of envying that mighty power of phantasy
which was capable of turning a fairly common experience
into something so great and beautiful.

(Schopenhauer, *The Wisdom of Life*, translated by
T. Bailey Saunders, 12)

Byron knew that about himself:

I won't describe; description is my "forte,"
But every fool describes in these bright days
His wondrous journey to some foreign court,
And spawns his quarto, and demands your praise –
Death to his publisher, to him 't is sport;
While Nature, tortured twenty thousand ways,
Resigns herself with exemplary patience
To guide-book, rhymes, tours, sketches, illustrations.

(*Don Juan*, V, 52)

Schopenhauer would focus on Byron's creative achievements and
refuse to waste time contemplating any of the typecast images of the
poet, such as "Rousseau – Goethe – Young – Aretino – Timon of
Athens ... Satan – Shakespeare – Bonaparte – Tiberius ... Henry the
8th – ... Chenier – ... Mirabeau ... Michael Angelo – ... [or]
Raphael." (Quoted by Christiansen, 201.) Hazlitt's assertion that
Byron "is, in a striking degree, the creature of his own will" is a
more accurate aperçu. The following passage from Byron's *Detached
Thoughts* (1821-1822), demonstrates the poet's firm sense of self-
containment as a man and as a writer:

I can't see any point of resemblance: [Rousseau] wrote prose,
I verse: he was of the people, I of the Aristocracy: he was a
philosopher, I am none: he published his first work at forty, I
mine at eighteen: his first essay brought him universal
applause, mine the contrary: he married his house-keeper, I
could not keep house with my wife: he thought all the world
in a plot against *him*, my little world seems to think *me* in a
plot against it, if I may judge by their abuse in print and coterie
...

9

Hazlitt, though piqued by it, corroborates Byron's self-image:

> He [Byron] holds no communion with his kind, but stands
> alone without mate or fellow –
>
>> 'As if a man were author of himself,
>> And owned no other kin.'
>
> He is like a solitary peak, all access to which is cut off not
> more by elevation than distance. He is seated on a lofty
> eminence, 'cloud-capt,' or reflecting the last rays of setting
> suns ...
>
> *(Spirit of the Age)*

Hazlitt's portrayal of the Lord, languorously energising his visions
with "the last rays of setting suns", is very different from his portrayal
of Wordsworth, whose poetry was, in Hazlitt's view, the result of a
much more sprightly process:

> It [Wordsworth's poetry] is one of the innovations of the time.
> It partakes of, and is carried along with, the revolutionary
> movement of our age: the political changes of the day were
> the model on which he formed and conducted his experiments
> ...
>
> *(Spirit of the Age)*

Hazlitt was able to admire what he called Wordsworth's "levelling"
muse, but he was unable to forgive Byron for "taking up ordinary
men and things in [his] hands with haughty indifference", and he
was unable to contain his irritation at Byron's maintaining such an
air of importance while writing for no cause. Byron wrote in his
Journal in 1814:

> As for me, by the blessing of indifference, I have simplified
> my politics into an utter detestation of all existing
> governments; and as it is the shortest and most agreeable and
> summary feeling imaginable, the first moment of an universal
> republic would convert me into an advocate for single and
> uncontradicted despotism. The fact is, riches are power, and
> poverty is slavery all over the earth, and one sort of
> establishment is no better, nor worse, for a *people* than another.

Later, the writing would evolve into something like a force of nature, a sort of versifying black hole, into which all the hypocrisy of the world is irresistibly drawn:

> And such as they are, such my present tale is,
> A nondescript and ever-varying rhyme,
> A versified Aurora Borealis,
> Which flashes o'er a waste and icy clime.
> When we know what all are, we must bewail us,
> But ne'ertheless I hope it is no crime
> To laugh at *all* things – for I wish to know
> *What*, after *all*, are *all* things – but a *show*?
>
> (*Don Juan*, VII, 2)

It was the apparent ease with which Byron could produce canto after electrifying canto that most annoyed those writers who could not. Tom Paulin has identified something about Hazlitt that goes some way to explaining the virulence of Hazlitt's critique of Byron:

> Hazlitt's sense of inferiority as a prose-writer emerges in his lecture 'On Poetry in General', where he speaks of the "jerks, the breaks, the inequalities, and harshness of prose", which destroy the flow of poetic imagination, as "a jolting road or stumbling horse disturbs the reverie of an absent man". He is saying that there is something gauche, thrawn, lumpish, dissonant – even downright annoying – about prose ... prose and plodding [may be] linked ...
>
> (*The Day-Star of Liberty:*
> *William Hazlitt's Radical Style*, 1998)

In Paulin's view, Hazlitt is working to contain an element of bitterness about what he suspects is his intractably second-rate nature: even if he achieves his goal in becoming the best prose writer of his time, Hazlitt will never be one of the *noblesse oblige*. He will always occupy the sort of marginal, vaguely parasitical place in literature that critics are often perceived to occupy.

Shelley heard Byron recite Canto V of *Don Juan* in 1821, and wrote to tell his wife Mary about the experience. The letter reveals a Shelley who seems to have felt almost as if he had been caught up in a tropical storm, so buffeted was he by the ferocity of Byron's imagination:

It [*Don Juan*] sets him not above but far above all the poets of the day: every word has the stamp of immortality. – I despair of rivalling Lord Byron, as well I may: and there is no other with whom it is worth contending. This canto is in style, but totally, & sustained with incredible ease and power... there is not a word which the most rigid assertor of the dignity of human nature could desire to be cancelled ...

> (Shelley to Mary Shelley, 10th August 1821.
> Bodleian Library,
> University of Oxford, MS Shelley, c.1, fo. 443-8)

Shelley had himself been inspired to compose the ravishing poem, 'Ode to the West Wind', in the wind-lashed woods above Florence, in 1819:

> O WILD West Wind, thou breath of Autumn's being,
> Thou, from whose unseen presence the leaves dead
> Are driven, like ghosts from an enchanter fleeing,
>
> Yellow, and black, and pale, and hectic red,
> Pestilence-stricken multitudes: O Thou,
> Who chariotest to their dark wintry bed
>
> The winged seeds, where they lie cold and low,
> Each like a corpse within its grave, until
> Thine azure sister of the Spring shall blow
>
> Her clarion o'er the dreaming earth, and fill
> (Driving sweet buds like flocks to feed in air)
> With living hues and odours plain and hill:
>
> Wild Spirit, which art moving every-where;
> Destroyer and Preserver; hear, O hear!
>
> (1)
>
> Thou on whose stream, 'mid the steep sky's commotion,
> Loose clouds like Earth's decaying leaves are shed,
> Shook from the tangled boughs of Heaven and Ocean,
>
> Angels of rain and lightning: there are spread
> On the blue surface of thine aery surge,
> Like the bright hair uplifted from the head

Of some fierce Mænad, even from the dim verge
Of the horizon to the zenith's height,
The locks of the approaching storm. Thou Dirge

Of the dying year, to which this closing night
Will be the dome of a vast sepulchre,
Vaulted with all thy congregated might

Of vapours, from whose solid atmosphere
Black rain, and fire, and hail, will burst: O hear!

(2)

It is impressive to think that the author of the above lines was himself
impressed with Byron's *Don Juan*, Canto V, which included the
following stanzas:

The European with the Asian shore
Sprinkled with palaces – the Ocean stream:
Here and there studded with a seventy-four,
Sophia's Cupola with golden gleam,
The cypress groves, Olympus high and hoar,
The twelve isles, and the more than I could dream,
Far less describe, present the very view
Which charmed the charming Mary Montague.

(V, 3)

The wind swept down the Euxine, and the wave
Broke foaming o'er the blue Symplegades;
'T is a grand sight from off "the Giant's Grave"
To watch the progress of those rolling seas
Between the Bosphorus, as they lash and lave
Europe and Asia, you being quite at ease:
There's not a sea the passenger e'er pukes in,
Turns up more dangerous breakers than the Euxine.

(V, 5)

'Twas a raw day of Autumn's bleak beginning,
When nights are equal, but not so the days;
The Parcæ then cut short the further spinning
Of seamen's fates, and the loud tempests raise
The waters, and repentance for past sinning
In all, who o'er the great deep take their ways:

> They vow to amend their lives, and yet they don't;
> Because if drowned, they can't – if spared, they won't.
>
> (V, 6)

Like Shelley, Byron, too, can conjure the wind and rain to agitate his stanzas, as if from within them. But one further thing about Byron's poetry that Shelley envied was the humour. The last two lines above serve as a good example. They demonstrate the humorous neatness with which Byron could give readers an instantly recognisable sense of their morals' absurd elasticity. Shelley was never able to infuse his poetry with such regular lightning-touches as that. He did try. In 'Peter Bell the Third' (1819), for instance, the mask of humour slid straight off the physiognomy of Shelley's serious style, as he tried to attack Wordsworth ('Peter'):

> But from the first 'twas Peter's drift
> To be a kind of moral eunuch,
> He touched the hem of Nature's shift,
> Felt faint – and never dared uplift
> The closest, all-concealing tunic.
>
> (Part the Fourth)

The above is rather clever, and it is clear enough how Shelley meant it to be humorous – but does it make the reader feel mirth? Being a loose cannon of a poet (whereas Shelley was a self-professed improver of mankind) liberated Byron, making humour more likely, and frequent:

> She snatched it, and refused another morsel,
> Saying he had gorged enough to make a horse ill.
>
> (*Don Juan*, II, 159)

Shelley tried and tried to draw from the same well that nourished Byron's work, without becoming contaminated by Byron's "full Hell/ Within" (as Shelley wrote, in 1818, in 'Julian and Maddalo'). In 'The Witch of Atlas', another of Shelley's attempts to reach Byron's wide audience, not one drop of funniness is able to make it through Shelley's impenetrable idiom:

The king would dress an ape up in his crown
And robes, and seat him on his glorious seat,
And on the right hand of the sunlike throne
Would place a gaudy mock-bird to repeat
The chatterings of the monkey. – Every one
Of the prone courtiers crawled to kiss the feet
Of their great Emperor when the morning came;
And kissed – alas, how many kiss the same!

(84)

While there is no automatic justification for comparing Shelley's
work unfavourably with Byron's, it is worth noting that Johann
Wolfgang von Goethe (1749-1832) recognised in Byron's humour
the key to his greatness as a poet:

> *Don Juan* is a work of boundless genius, manifesting the
> bitterest and most savage hatred of humanity, and then again
> penetrated with the deepest and tenderest love for mankind.
> And as we already know and esteem the author and would
> not have him other than he is, we gratefully enjoy what the
> excessive licence, nay with audacity, he dares to set before
> us. The technical handling of the verse is quite in harmony
> with the strange, wild, ruthless content; the poet spares his
> language as little as he spares humanity; and as we approach
> closer we become aware that English poetry is already in
> possession of something we Germans totally lack: a cultured
> comic language.
>
> (Translated and quoted by E.M. Butler in
> *Byron and Goethe* [1956], 49)

Goethe attributes Byron's funniness to his Englishness, but, given
the unfunniness of fellow English poet, Shelley, it may be worth
considering T.S. Eliot's (1888-1965) suggestion that Byron is in fact
a Scottish poet:

> This is not the satire of Dryden, still less of Pope ... This is
> not indeed English satire at all; it is really a *flyting* [a 'scolding-
> match'], and closer in feeling and intention to the satire of
> [William] Dunbar:

Lene larbar, loungeour, baith lowsy in lisk and loye;
Fy! Skolderit skyn, thou art both skyre and strumple ...
[Lean, impotent weakling, lounger, lousy in both groin
    and loin;
Fie! scorched skin, you are both scratched and wrinkled ...]
                (*On Poetry and Poets* [1957])

Byron was *flyting* when he said, at the very beginning of *Don Juan*:

You, Bob [Southey]! are rather insolent, you know,
At being disappointed in your wish
To supersede all warblers here below,
And be the only Blackbird in the dish;
And then you overstrain yourself, or so,
And tumble downward like the flying fish
Gasping on deck, because you soar too high, Bob,
And fall, for lack of moisture, quite a-dry, Bob!
                            (Dedication, 3)

Hurling sexual innuendoes across the glen at his literary
adversaries was not the only funny thing Byron could do. In the
following passage, from a little later in *Don Juan* (I), the reader
witnesses the shape-shifting of the Byronic sense of humour, which
becomes, as each new narrative perspective opens out, more powerful,
compacted, and complicated (and naughtier) than may so easily be
explained by the poet's provenance:

Wedded she was some years, and to a man
Of fifty, and such husbands are in plenty;
And yet, I think, instead of such a ONE
'Twere better to have TWO of five-and-twenty,
Especially in countries near the sun:
And now I think on 't, "*mi vien in mente*,"
Ladies even of the most uneasy virtue
Prefer a spouse whose age is short of thirty.
                            (I, 62)

'Tis a sad thing, I cannot choose but say,
And all the fault of that indecent sun,
Who cannot leave alone our helpless clay,
But will keep baking, broiling, burning on,

That howsoever people fast and pray,
The flesh is frail, and so the soul undone:
What men call gallantry, and gods adultery,
Is much more common where the climate's sultry.

(I, 63)

Happy the nations of the moral North!
Where all is virtue, and the winter season
Sends sin, without a rag on, shivering forth
('Twas snow that brought St Anthony to reason);
Where juries cast up what a wife is worth
By laying whate'er sum, in mulct, they please on
The lover, who must pay a handsome price,
Because it is a marketable vice.

(I, 64)

There is the sense in which Byron pulled magically coruscating cotton off the reel of his genius, and he did it endlessly. (*Don Juan* was nowhere near finished at the time of Byron's death.) His presence to his contemporaries was something like as disheartening as the existence of Marcel Proust (1871-1922) – whose long novel, *À la recherche du temps perdu*, deals with the relationship of the narrator to themes such as art, time, memory and society – would later be to Virginia Woolf (1882-1941), as she, talented in her own right, struggled to assert her own voice:

> Proust so titillates my own desire for expression that I can hardly set out the sentence. "Oh, if I could write like that!" I cry. And at the moment such is the astonishing [remember how Shelley called *Don Juan*, Canto V, "astonishingly fine"] vibration and saturation that he procures – there's something sexual in it – that I feel I *can* write like that, and seize my pen, and then I *can't* write like that.

Just as it was for Shelley writing to his wife about Canto V of Byron's *Don Juan*, the above passage from Woolf at first seems like a celebration of a great artist's work, but it is actually a far darker verdict on her own future as a writer. To read a work by either Proust or Byron, to witness the brilliant associative connections and sudden insights carried on the crisscrossing network of digressions, is to feel its presence as, in some sense, a form of life evolved independently in the artist's mind, and certainly "not [just] derived from books", as Ernest Hartley Coleridge would say in his introductory memoir to *The Poetical Works of Lord Byron* (1905).

Byron composed at tremendous speed. He began to compose *The Corsair: A Tale* on 16th October 1813; and having written 200 lines a day he completed the first draft by 27th October 1813. The poem was published on 1st February 1814, and sold 10,000 copies on that date. It was reprinted five times in the first month and six times more by the end of the next month. Byron achieved verbally something akin to what Napoleon Bonaparte (1769-1821) achieved militarily. When Hazlitt called Byron's spirit "fiery, impatient, wayward, indefatigable", he could just as easily have been describing the spirit of his (and Byron's) greatest hero, Napoleon. And when Hazlitt said that "Lord Byron's verse glows like a flame, consuming everything in its way", he could just as easily have been describing Napoleon's battle campaign. (Just substitute the name Napoleon for Byron, and the word "army" for "verse".) Napoleon gathered together a force of professional fighters and arrogantly dominated a France bleary-eyed with post-revolutionary exhaustion; so (in the realm of poetry), Byron would assert the supremacy of his own individual will in a depleted England. He wrote to Lady Melbourne in September 1813:

> 'Tis said – *Indifference* marks the present time
> Then hear the reason – though 'tis told in rhyme –
> A King who *can't* – a Prince of Wales who *don't* –
> Patriots who *shan't* – Ministers who *won't* –
> What matters who are *in* or *out* of place
> The *Mad* – the *Bad* – the *Useless* or the *Base*?

Much later, Byron would still be delineating English society with undulled alacrity:

> Our ridicules are kept in the back-ground –
> Ridiculous enough, but also dull;
> Professions, too, are no more to be found
> Professional; and there is nought to cull
> Of Folly's fruit; for though your fools abound,
> They're barren, and not worth the pains to pull.

Society is now one polished horde,
Formed of two mighty tribes, the *Bores* and *Bored*.

(*Don Juan*, XIII, 95)

In one sense Byron saw that the country was a great lump of butter. He knew he could be the knife. He wrote *The Corsair* in, as Michael Schmidt puts it, "a headlong heroic couplet measure in which [he] took ironic liberties with the dynamic and the traditions of the form." (Penguin Poetry First Editions.)

Byron's stylistic looseness seems (as he meant it to seem) a sure symptom of the defiant intellect that will leap intuitively rather than analyse exhaustively ("poetry is in itself passion, and does not systematize. It assails, but does not argue; it may be wrong, but it does not assume pretensions to Optimism." [*Letters and Journals*, V, 582]) That looseness allowed for Byron's startling deployment of enjambment – "BOB SOUTHEY! You're a poet – Poet laureate,/ And representative of all the race;/Although 'tis true that you turn'd out a Tory at/Last ..." (*Don Juan*, Dedication, 1) – and wholly unexpected rhymes: "But – Oh! ye lords of ladies intellectual,/Inform us truly have they not hen-peck'd you all?" (*Don Juan*, I, 21). There is such sheer arrogance in the apparent lack of attention to detail. The narrator of *Don Juan* claims to know:

> ... some words of Spanish, Turk, and Greek,
> Italian not at all, having no teachers;
> Much English I cannot pretend to speak,
> Learning that language chiefly from its preachers,
> Barrow, South, Tillotson, whom every week
> I study, also Blair – the highest reachers
> Of eloquence in piety and prose –
> I hate your poets, so read none of those.

(II, 165)

Byron has no problem in posing as a foreigner in order to offend those English readers who aspire to live their lives in accordance with the writings of popular theologians and preachers (Barrow, South and Tillotson). While other poets applied their words and phrases with a sense of sacred care, Byron disrespectfully splashed, sloshed, spilled and swilled the surfeit of his muse. He occasionally expressed remorse about the way he wrote. He confessed to Thomas Moore (later his biographer) that it had only taken him ten days to write *The Corsair*, "which I take to be the most humiliating confession, as it proves my own want of judgement in publishing, and the public's in reading things, which cannot have stamina for permanent attention."

Shelley, for whom (in his essay, 'A Defence of Poetry' [1821]) true poets were "the Hierophants of an unapprehended inspiration, compelled to serve the power which is seated in the throne of their own soul", confided his belief in a letter to Thomas Love Peacock (1785-1866) in July 1816 that "[Byron] is a slave to the vilest and most vulgar prejudices". Hazlitt also called Byron a "pamperer of the public's prejudices". In the light of those views, it seems that Byron was not as interested as Shelley in using his imagination as "The great instrument of moral good"; nor was he as interested as Shelley in "defeat[ing] the curse which binds us to be subjected to the accident of surrounding impressions" ('A Defence of Poetry'). Moore knew Byron extremely well, so his claim that Byron found "consecutive ratiocination" disagreeable is to be taken seriously. In 1827, Byron's banker friend Douglas Kinnaird noted that there was "a great deal of the woman" about Byron's way of thinking, including "his tenderness, his temper, his caprice, his vanity". Chapter 5 of Stabler's *Byron, Poetics and History* (2002) demonstrates how *Don Juan*, in Stabler's view, "feminises digressive activity" (150), Byron taking up the "feminine" privilege of capriciousness and inconstancy. One thinks of Shakespeare's Cleopatra, so enchanting and disturbing, that quintessence of femininity by whom Mark Antony and Enobarbus were, in their different ways, beguiled and confounded. Act I of *Antony and Cleopatra* showcases Cleopatra's unpredictable combination of skittishness and cruelty, and concludes with the quiet shock of her half-threat to "unpeople Egypt" if she does not get her way. Similarly, Byron's poetry beguiled and confounded readers by jumping unpredictably from one narrative point of view to another. "'Tis time we should return to plain narration" (*Don Juan*, VI, 57), says Byron, having 'digressed', only to digress again into the trivial subject of ladies' hairpins, before interrupting himself again with a lunge at bigger issues:

> But these are foolish things to all the wise,
> And I love Wisdom more than she loves me;

My tendency is to philosophize [yet in Canto X he *"won't*
  philosophize"]
On most things, from a tyrant to a tree;
But still the spouseless virgin *Knowledge* flies
What are we? and whence came we? what shall be
Our *ultimate* existence? what's our present?
Are questions answerless, and yet incessant.

(*Don Juan*, VI, 63)

In *Don Juan* the narrator is the figure who raises readers up and
knocks them down. The narrator is always interfering, like a Tristram
Shandy (In the writing of *The Life and Opinions of Tristram Shandy,
Gentleman* [1760-7], Laurence Sterne [1713-68] eschewed the
popular devices of linear narrative and epistolary structure, and in
so doing he implied that the artifice of these forms bears little relation
to the reality of human experience):

But then the fact's a fact – and 'tis the part
Of a true poet to escape from fiction
Whene'er he can; for there is little art
In leaving verse more free from the restriction
Of Truth than prose, unless to suit the mart
For what is sometimes called poetic diction,
And that outrageous appetite for lies
Which Satan angles with for souls, like flies.

(*Don Juan*, VIII, 86)

The narrative is never straightforward, and it is always at an oblique
angle to the main subject. It is a modern reading experience to not
know where one is as a reader, and to experience the ready confusion
between author and subject. In the following example, there is some
intriguing philosophical speculation about what thought actually is,
but that enquiry is shoved aside by the vulgarly assertive ego:

I won't describe, – that is, if I can help
Description; and I won't reflect, – that is,
If I can stave off thought, which – as a whelp
Clings to its teat – sticks to me through the abyss
Of this cold labyrinth; or as the kelp
Holds by the rock; or as a lover's kiss

Drains its first draught of lips: – but, as I said,
I *won't* philosophize, and *will* be read.

(Don Juan, X, 28)

Byron's ostentatious avowal of base sentiments, irreverently intermeshed with hiccups of high seriousness, made him a problem for many readers. The grotesqueness, violence and ridiculousness of the following passage from *Don Juan* illustrates the point:

A dying Moslem, who had felt the foot
Of a foe o'er him, snatched at it, and bit
The very tendon which is most acute –
(That which some ancient Muse or modern wit
Named after thee, Achilles!) and quite through't
He made the teeth meet, nor relinquished it
Even with his life – for (but they lie) 'tis said
To the live leg still clung the severed head.

(VIII, 84)

However this may be, 't is pretty sure
The Russian officer for life was lamed,
For the Turk's teeth stuck faster than a skewer,
And left him 'midst the invalid and maimed:
The regimental surgeon could not cure
His patient, and, perhaps, was to be blamed
More than the head of the inveterate foe,
Which was cut off, and scarce even then let go.

(VIII, 85)

Byron was more like the hierophant of mischief, rather than Shelley's "hierophant … of an unapprehended inspiration" with a "passion for reforming the world" ('A Defence of Poetry').

Francis Hodgson was shocked by what he, and many others, saw as the immorality of *Childe Harold*. Hodgson perceived Byron's spirituality to be in a perilous state. But Hodgson had, a year earlier than the publication of *Childe Harold*, already read in a letter Byron's thoughts about conventional Christianity:

I will have nothing to do with your immortality; we are miserable enough in this life, without the absurdity of speculating upon another. If men are to live, why die at all?

and if they die, why disturb the sweet and sound sleep that 'knows no waking'? ... As to revealed religion, Christ came to save men; but a good Pagan will go to heaven, and a bad Nazarene to hell ... why are not all men Christians? or why are any? If mankind may be saved who never heard or dreamt, at Timbuctoo, Otaheite, Terra Incognita, etc., of Galilee and its Prophet, Christianity is of no avail ... (September 1811)

Byron "had an instinctive knowledge of how to market himself" (Grosskurth, 57), and had been marketing himself with increasing sophistication since telling Robert Charles Dallas in January 1808 that he had "been already held up as a votary of Licentiousness and the Disciple of Infidelity". By September 1811, a few months before the publication of *Childe Harold's Pilgrimage* I and II, he was spreading the word that he was (if he *must* be like something) like an anti-messiah come to disabuse people of the false expectations instilled in them by the teachings of Jesus Christ. Byron is, he tells Hodgson, "no Platonist ... nothing at all" (September 1811). He remains at loggerheads with the majority who prefer to believe in something (although the majority of them have made their preference by deceiving themselves). He will certainly not try to perfect his readers. Later still, in the 1820s, the cantos of *Don Juan* – a never-ending cataract of negatives and nay saying – will be pouring out of him: he "*won't* philosophize", and when he "*will*" do anything, he will amuse his readers with tales of, say, adultery (the negative of matrimony) and cannibalism (the negative of human kindness). In his essay, 'Byron's Bad English', Charles LaChance argues very persuasively that Byron's prosody and style reinforce nihilism in his revolt against the four major belief systems of Western culture: Rousseauist sentimentality, platonised Christianity, masculinist heroics and scientific or empirical naturalism. In LaChance's view:

Unmitigated nihilism occurs when all these received ideologies are radically subverted, implying no universal or objective basis is knowable by which any system could be finally favoured. Such nihilism infuses Lord Byron's *Don Juan*. Here, philosophical nihil originates in a cycle of Weltanschauungs mutually undercutting and contradicting each other in various burlesque adventures on battlefield and bed.

LaChance's exegesis is liberally dotted with pointers to, and explanations of, the function of the specific tools in Byron's weaponry:

> Like all revolutions, Byron's requires bad language ... Negative grammar, lewd diction, discordant phonology, motley syntax and erotic tropes delineates his style. Specifically, women's alleged inconstancy and imagery of the vagina are governing metaphors marking the abyss of Byronic nihility.
>
> (*English*, volume 50, number 197, Summer 2001)

It could be argued that Byron's sole aim as a satirist is to hit society when it misbehaves (all the time), and to hit it hard. It could be argued that he is not interested in improving society by correcting its behaviour in the way a spiritual leader would. His observations end in nothing:

> It is an awful topic – but 'tis not
> My cue for any time to be terrific:
> For checkered as is seen our human lot
> With good, and bad, and worse, alike prolific
> Of melancholy merriment, to quote
> Too much of one sort would be soporific;–
> Without, or with, offence to friends or foes,
> I sketch your world exactly as it goes.
>
> (*Don Juan*, VIII, 89)

He leaves the reader in the lurch. His pessimism is no different from that expounded on in the Scriptures (which the nurse, May Gray, thrashed into the nine-year-old Byron when she was not sexually abusing him): "Verily it is a wretched thing to be alive on the earth!" Furthermore, it could be argued that Wordsworth and Coleridge at least tried to explain the origins and causes of human folly and suffering, and they tried to offer remedies. They were not satisfied with giving their readers spiritual consultations only. They wanted to treat them and cure them ("nourish" and "repair" them, as Wordsworth, in collaboration with Coleridge, argued in *The Prelude* [1850]). Byron, however, after clearly showing readers that the complaint they suffer from is incurable, turns his back on them with a sardonic grin ...

That argument, however easy it is to understand and believe, is wrong. Like Samuel Johnson's (1709-1784) in *The Vanity of Human Wishes*, Byron's voice is extremely serious but, importantly, the high seriousness is never in danger of being toppled by the low humour with which it necessarily coexists in the Byronic vision. The fibre of the vision is much too tough to be undone by the humorous twists. The humorous twists form an integral part of the process of building the Byronic vision. In the following stanza, the shipwrecked, and famished, Don Juan is nursed back to health by Zoe, whose illiteracy has not stopped her from knowing things:

> He ate, and he was well supplied; and she,
> Who watched him like a mother, would have fed
> Him past all bounds, because she smiled to see
> Such appetite in one she had deemed dead:
> But Zoe, being older than Haidée,
> Knew (by tradition, for she ne'er had read)
> That famished people must be slowly nurst,
> And fed by spoonfuls, else they always burst.
>
> > (*Don Juan*, II, 158)

Byron has Haidée teach Don Juan her language "by dint of fingers and of eyes,/And words repeated after her", and there is an effectiveness about such direct education which is – the exiled poet implies – preferable to (English) artificiality:

> Thus Juan learned his *alpha beta* better
> From Haidée's glance than any graven letter.
>
> > (*Don Juan*, II, 163)

Just as Johnson had, "with extensive view/Survey[ed] mankind", and found time after time that "rarely reason guides" human beings' decision-making processes in matters great or small, so Byron, having traced humans' "path[s] ... through perplexing ways", can confront canting morality and say that it is a "pity ... that/Pleasure's a sin, and sometimes Sin's a pleasure" (*Don Juan*, I, 133). He can get right under the skin of society and lay bare the interchangeable dynamics of its hypocrisy:

'Tis strange, – but true; for Truth is always strange –
Stranger than fiction: if it could be told,
How much would novels gain by the exchange!
How differently the World would men behold!
How oft would Vice and Virtue places change!
The new world would be nothing to the old,
If some Columbus of the moral seas
Would show mankind their soul's antipodes.

(Don Juan, XV, 101)

Like Johnson, Byron has the capacity to include the panorama of humanity in his vision, and he also has the motivation to examine every manifestation of humans' connective disease. There could not be a more serious theme. Paradoxically, there could not be more potential for comedy. In Byron's (as in Johnson's) hands, the mix is potent. The Victorian poet, essayist and literary critic, Matthew Arnold (1822-88), would explain Byron's uniqueness, or, more accurately, his unique seriousness:

> In spite of his prodigious vogue, Byron has never yet ... had the serious admiration which he deserves ... Even of his passionate admirers, how many never got beyond the theatrical Byron, from which they caught the fashion of deranging their hair, or of knotting back their neck-handkerchief, or of leaving their shirt-collar unbuttoned; how few profoundly felt his vital influence, the influence of his splendid and imperishable excellence of sincerity and strength!

Arnold continues with critical writing that is a powerful blend of rigour and sympathy, giving a sense of how unpropitious the *zeitgeist* was to Byron's endeavours:

> [Byron's] own aristocratic class, whose cynical make-believe drove him to fury; the great middle-class, on whose impregnable Philistinism he shattered himself to pieces, – how little have either of these felt Byron's vital influence! As the inevitable break-up of the old order comes, as the English middle-class slowly awakens from its intellectual sleep of two centuries, as our actual present world, to which this sleep has condemned us, shows itself more clearly, – our world of an aristocracy materialised and null, a middle-class purblind and

hideous, a lower class crude and brutal, – we shall turn our eyes again, and to more purpose, upon this passionate and dauntless soldier of forlorn hope, who, ignorant of the future and unconsoled by its promises, nevertheless waged against the conservation of the old impossible world ...

(Preface to Arnold's edition of Byron's poetry [1881])

The French novelist Gustave Flaubert (1821-80), most famous for *Madame Bovary* (1857), for which he was prosecuted (and acquitted) on charges of immorality, would appreciate Byron's position:

Really I profoundly value only two men, Rabelais and Byron, the only two who have written in a spirit of malice toward the human race and with the intention of laughing in its face. What a tremendous position a man occupies who places himself in such a relation to the world!

(to Ernest Chevalier, September, 1838)

Of course, Byron himself had always been capable of saying that kind of thing for himself (though – as Byron knew – few were really listening):

And one good action in the midst of crimes
Is "quite refreshing," in the affected phrase
Of these ambrosial, Pharisaic times,
With all their pretty milk-and-water ways,
And may serve therefore to bedew these rhymes,
A little scorched at present with the blaze
Of conquest and its consequences, which
Make Epic poesy so rare and rich.

(*Don Juan*, VIII, 90)

In Phyllis Grosskurth's view, Byron was "Sceptical, impious, misanthropic [and] spoke of women with contempt and railed against family life", and he had "no real friends, simply companions" (Grosskurth, 76). Peter Quennell has noted that:

Madame de Staël was somewhat exasperated by the poet's sleepy and supercilious manners, his habit of sitting at dinner with his eyes half shut, and the dreadful blasphemies he presumed to utter against love. He was "totally *in*sensible to *la belle passion*", she declared, in the course of a vociferous attack delivered over a dinner table, and *had* been all his life ... "*C'est un demon!*" she cried...

(Byron: The Years of Fame, 135)

In everyday matters he allowed himself to live badly – not just badly to others, but badly to himself. With regard to his eating habits, he was:

Caught in a vicious circle of indulgence and abstinence [and] he would devour a heavy meal, generally of vegetables and fish, only to be visited by ... hideous nightmares that left him sweating and shaken – wild dreams in which the dead returned to pursue – or open his eyes to the agonies of a bilious headache. It is not surprising that his liver was often recalcitrant, that he suffered from fits of spleen and depression ...

(Byron: The Years of Fame, 164)

The reason for all the inwardly and outwardly directed badness was that he considered it a matter of the utmost urgency "to feel that we exist – even through pain." (*Letters and Journals* III, 109). The monotony of eating correctly and treating everyone politely was not to be tolerated. Life – *feeling* life – was too short:

When one subtracts from life infancy (which is vegetation), sleep, eating, and swilling – buttoning and unbuttoning – how much remains of downright existence? The summer of a dormouse.

(quoted by Quennell, 164.)

Byron sharply defined his preference for sensation over monotony in his *Detached Thoughts* (October 1821-May 1822):

33

I have a notion that Gamblers are as happy as most people, being always *excited*. Women, wine, fame, the table, even Ambition, *sate* [cloy] now and then; but every turn of the card, and cast of the dice, keeps the Gamester alive: besides one can game ten times longer than one can do any thing else.

As Doris Langley-Moore puts it, Byron, in his "desire for dominance" had "a kind of intuitive ... authority, springing from the conviction of having a right to be entirely [him]self." (*Lord Byron: Accounts Rendered*, 149). He allowed glimpses of his sexual predilections into his letters. He wrote to Henry Drury in June 1809, projecting an essay on "Sodomy simplified or Paederasty proved to be praiseworthy from ancient authors and modern practice." It would be a long, long time before such candour would be accepted by a homophobic and hypocritical English society. The classical scholar and educator, Benjamin Jowett (1817-93), would translate Plato's (?427-?347 B.C.) *Phaedrus*, but it would require all Jowett's ingenuity to rephrase Plato's depiction of paederastia into the affectionate regard as exists between an Englishman and his wife.

If, like Coleridge and Shelley, Byron believed in the ubiquitous creativity of human consciousness, he allowed the sulphurous vapours from his troubled conscience equal ubiquity. In Anthony Fowles' view, John Dryden's (1631-1700) "objectivity gave him a place to stand and hence leverage", enabling him, "Just apart from, just above, the fray [to] anatomise with the nicest discrimination" (*John Dryden*, xviii). Byron's case was different from Dryden's in that, although he too found the "place to stand and hence leverage", he found it *in himself*: he looked his own demons square in the face. Knowing intuitively that those demons are contained and concealed (even discarded) by all members of all classes of English civilisation, Byron chose instead to consult with them. As in any war, one must, however unpalatable the idea, communicate at some stage with the enemy. The finished products of Byron's life and work are shot through with the frank observations of personal demons:

> ... there is a fire
> And motion of the Soul which will not dwell
> In its own narrow being, but aspire
> Beyond the fitting medium of desire;
> And, but once kindled, quenchless evermore,
> Preys ...
>
> (*Childe Harold's Pilgrimage*, III, 42)

In that respect, Byron's vision has a surprising affinity with that of a poet whose transfigured view of the world ensured his almost total obscurity: William Blake (1757-1827). Each of Blake's works is part of what he called, in the Preface to his poem, *Milton*, his "Mental Fight" to unthink the assumptions of conventional (and corrupt) wisdom. Blake made the fullest and most uncompromising statement in rejecting the materialism promoted by the philosophy of Francis Bacon (1561-1626), Sir Isaac Newton (1642-1727) and John Locke (1632-1704) that was coming into its full power at the time Blake was at work:

> The Stolen and Perverted Writings of Homer & Ovid, of Plato & Cicero, which all Men ought to contemn, are set up by artifice …
>
> Rouze up, O Young Men of the New Age! set your foreheads against the ignorant Hirelings! For we have Hirelings in the Camp, the Court & the University, who would, if they could, for ever depress Mental & prolong Corporeal War. Painters! on you I call. Sculptors! Architects! Suffer not the fashionable Fools to depress your powers by the prices they pretend to give for contemptible works, or the expensive advertizing boasts that they make of such works …
>
> (Written and etched in 1804-1808)

Byron did not make, like Blake, a lifelong effort to "buil[d] Jerusalem/ In England …", but he often fired broadsides packed with all the eloquence and impatience of radical thinking:

> the madmen who have made men mad
> By their contagion; Conquerors and kings,
> Founders of sects and systems, to whom add
> Sophists, Bards, Statesmen, all unquiet things
> Which stir too strongly the soul's secret springs …

Byron did think that it would be best to "unteach Mankind the lust to shine or rule" (*Childe Harold's Pilgrimage*, III, 43), but he did not want that thought to become part of a sect or system of *his*: he just thought, and uttered, it, shedding the grace of his genius over it, before moving on to the next thing.

Like an unusually agile child on a climbing frame, Byron had fun amongst words, and his poetry often communicates joy. He exploited to the full both the value of lyrical hyperbole:

His mother was a learnéd lady, famed
For every branch of every science known –
In every Christian language ever named,
With virtues equalled by her wit alone:
She made the cleverest people quite ashamed,
And even the good with inward envy groan,
Finding themselves so very much exceeded,
In their own way, by all the things that she did.

(Don Juan, I, 10)*

and suggestive understatement:

Yet Julia's very coldness still was kind,
And tremulously gentle her small hand
Withdrew itself from his, but left behind
A little pressure, thrilling, and so bland
And slight, so very sight, that to the mind
'T was but a doubt; but ne'er magician's wand
Wrought change with all Armida's fairy art
Like what this light touch left on Juan's heart.

(Don Juan, I, 71)*

Although it may be possible to postulate a formal classification of Byron's poetry, any schematising attempts invariably simplify the complex and subtle interweaving of moods and techniques. A single passage of a few lines may move from a moment of intense lyricism to a passage of sharp analysis or deflating irony, but Byron's imagination created a context and a psychology for all the modulations. The results were saleable. People saw in Byron's poetry their own despised and discarded thoughts returning to them with revivified splendour. Byron was the biggest-selling author of his day, completely outshining Walter Scott (1771-1832) who had been the biggest-selling writer up until then. Byron's impact on society did not, as Oscar Wilde (1854-1900) would say so shrewdly in 1891, "intensify [his] strength" but rather "exaggerate[d his] weakness." By 1816, society was scandalised by the rumours that Byron had committed "Sodomy ... the vilest crime possible, punishable by death, and the culprit was hanged on a separate gallows so as not to contaminate the other criminals." (Grosskurth, 267.) The Rev. William Harness thought that Byron had a "morbid love of a bad reputation" (*The Literary Life of the Rev. William Harness*, 21). Just as Thomas De Quincey (1785-1859) fashioned himself as part of the literary product he created, by alternately glamorising and reviling his addiction to opium in *Confessions of an English Opium-Eater* (1821), so Byron "dramatised every situation in which he played a leading part ... If he were to be disgraced, he must play the role to the hilt." (Grosskurth, 267.)

Byron became a bad husband on the day of his marriage, rather than allowing any "Optimism" about human nature (his or his wife's) to delay the inevitable deterioration in happiness (or spoil the opportunity to employ zeugma): "I got a wife and a cold on the same day, but have got rid of the last pretty speedily", he told Lady Melbourne in January 1815. By December 1815, when Byron's wife Annabella was giving birth to Augusta Ada, Byron was shooting his pistols in the room below. He may have been jealous of the new arrival: the presence of a baby, trailing clouds of glory and filling nappies regularly, would no doubt interfere with Annabella's remaining enthusiasm for her husband, an only child. But Byron was frequently violent before and after the birth of his daughter. He often smashed his own prized possessions (though biographers Phyllis Grosskurth and Fiona McCarthy reassure us that he never touched his wife). That violence was the less beguiling physical manifestation of the mind behind his greatest works. He cut his swathe through books, experiences and people, subordinating them all to his requirements as a creative writer. His mind was strong enough to master it all, to assimilate and incorporate it with the flow of his thinking, and so to make it fit in with the unity of his insight, which, though huge, was always growing. In the process, his own thinking always dominated and was never drowned by others' thinking. Langley-Moore has tidily explicated the difference between Lord and Lady Byron on their separation "after a year of lacerating incompatibility" (*Accounts Rendered*, 215):

> In the end, Lady Byron proved the more grievously hurt. He had resilience, she almost none. He was self-critical and, in acknowledging 'the nightmare of my own delinquencies', could in some measure purge them. She was self-admiring, and contemplated with ever renewed amazement the transcendent injustice of her ill-usage, feeling more and more

virtuous, more and more wronged, as the years went by. He was able to distil from his experiences new materials, new ideas about life ...

(Accounts Rendered, 216)

One thing that Byron learned to do as a writer was to preserve the fluidity of his thinking without trying to 'unify' it, or justify it for absolutists:

> "*Que scais-je?*" [*what do I know?*] was the motto of
> Montaigne,
> As also of the first academicians:
> That all is dubious which man may attain,
> Was one of their most favourite positions.
> There's no such thing as certainty, that's plain
> As any of Mortality's conditions;
> So little do we know what we'er about in
> This world, I doubt if doubt itself be doubting.

(Don Juan, IX, 17)

The historian George Finlay made a creditable attempt to portray the inner-conflict beneath the unpredictable nature of Byron's behaviour and his poetry:

> It seemed as if two different souls occupied his body alternately. One was feminine, and full of sympathy; the other masculine, and characterized by clear judgment, and by a rare power of presenting for consideration those facts only which were required for forming a decision. When one arrived the other departed. In company, his sympathetic soul was his tyrant. Alone, or with a single person, his masculine prudence displayed itself as his friend. No man could then arrange facts, investigate their causes, or examine their consequences, with more logical accuracy, or in a more practical spirit. Yet, in his most sagacious moment, the entrance of a third person would derange the order of his ideas – judgment fled, and sympathy, generally laughing, took its place. Hence he appeared in his conduct extremely capricious, while in his opinions he had really great firmness. He often, however, displayed a feminine turn for deception in trifles, while at the same time he possessed a feminine candour of soul, and a natural love of

truth, which made him often despise himself quite as much as he despised English fashionable society for what he called its brazen hypocrisy.

(A History of Greece, Vol. 6, 1877)

Some people suppose that the energy that drives the Byronic heroism of a Childe Harold or a Don Juan is generated by the existence of a real, cankering, secret of the author – Byron's "central iniquity", as the later poet, Francis Thompson (1859-1907), would argue in his essay, *Shelley* (written in 1889). In the light of the biographical evidence, such a view is hard to resist. The burning of Byron's memoirs (which may have contained many explicit, well-informed references to incest and sodomy) in the grate of John Murray's Albemarle Street drawing room (on 17th May 1824) has since become known as the event at which Byron's friends decided to protect his posthumous reputation.

Byron was fitfully candid. He told his unfortunate wife that he had "done that for which I can never forgive myself". Despite – or perhaps because of – Byron's telling her that on their wedding day, Annabella (née Milbanke) nerved herself to attempt to elicit the whole truth from her husband, but – the hot flush of his honesty now passed – he would only further add that "good women could know nothing" of his secrets. Readers of *Detached Thoughts*, however, may speculate with reasonable confidence: when Byron says "I never hear the word 'Clare' without a beating of the heart", he is not referring to Claire Clairmont, the mother of his child Allegra, but to the Earl of Clare, with whom he had a schoolboy love affair at Harrow. Byron had sexual relationships with many boys, including the 15-year-old Trinity chorister John Edleston. Lady Caroline Lamb, with whom Byron had a sexual relationship, used to dress up as a pageboy for Byron, and it was Caroline Lamb who, on finding her continuing attraction to Byron unrequited, spread gossip about Byron's penchant for sodomy.

A penchant for sodomy was, of course, nothing new. Fame for the sodomite was. The 2nd Earl of Rochester, John Wilmot (1647-80), the poet, wit and libertine who wrote love lyrics and bawdy verse, had been bisexual like Byron, and had a very direct and Anglo-Saxon way of referring to sex, and a reductive way of discussing interpersonal affairs:

Quoth the Duchess of Cleveland to counsellor Knight,
"I'd fain have a prick, knew I how to come by't.
I desire you'll be secret and give your advice:
Though cunt be not coy, reputation is nice.

"To some cellar in Sodom Your Grace must retire
Where porters with black-pots sit round a coal fire;
There open your case and Your Grace cannot fail
Of a dozen of pricks for a dozen of ale."

"Is't so?" quoth the Duchess. "Aye, by God!" quoth the whore.
"Then give me the key that unlocks the back door,
For I'd rather be fucked by porters and Carmen
Than thus be abused by Churchill and Jermyn."

('Song')

Rochester had the same kind of poetic ability as Byron, but Byron had it better. It is hard to imagine that Byron was not aware of his work.

This was the first era in English history in which there were many, many daily newspapers. Celebrity, in the modern sense, became possible. Byron was a very well-known figure. Inevitably, when he wrote a poem about some figure with a strange dark secret, people would wonder what the secret was. They would speculate that it was something to do with his marriage, and rumours spread quickly that he was having an affair with his half-sister, Augusta Leigh, whilst practically on his honeymoon with Annabella. Regency society was scandalised, and in this way Byron's work and his life became bound up together in the popular mind. But sodomy, unlike incest, was an offence beyond the pale, and still punishable in England by death. Byron had to leave England in 1816. He would never return. He became even more sharply defined as the romantic outsider, with the pariah's privilege of frank expression:

The consequence is, being of no party,
I shall offend all parties: – never mind!
My words, at least, are more sincere and hearty
Than if I sought to sail before the wind.
He who has nought to gain can have small art: he

Who neither wishes to be bound or bind,
May still expatiate freely, as will I,
Nor give my voice to slavery's jackal cry.

(*Don Juan*, IX, 26)

I will now concentrate more specifically on his poetic works, and try to make clear what it is about those works that makes him one of the greatest poets that ever lived.

3

Early Works

Having argued in 1807 that Wordsworth's "force and expression [wa]s that of a genuine poet, feeling as he wr[ote]" (*Letters and Journals*, I, 341), later that year, with the publication of *Hours of Idleness*, Byron would express his distaste at Wordsworth's automatic moralising and philosophising, and assert his right as a poet, and a man, to be human:

> The wise sometimes from Wisdom's ways depart;
> Can youth then hush the dictates of the heart?
> Precepts of prudence curb, but can't controul,
> The fierce emotions of the flowing soul.

Young Byron's reliance on the path beaten by Alexander Pope (1688-1744) is clear, particularly when one reads the following passage from Pope's *Essay on Criticism* (1711):

> True ease in writing comes from art, not chance,
> As those move easiest who have learn'd to dance.
> 'Tis not enough no harshness gives offence,
> The sound must seem an Echo to the sense;
> Soft is the strain when Zephyr gently blows,
> And the smooth stream in smoother numbers flows:
> But when loud surges lash the sounding shore,
> The hoarse, rough verse should like the torrent roar.

(2)

The embryonic Byronic imagination is, if not yet as rampant as it will be in *Don Juan*, certainly in an advanced state of vitality:

When Love's delirium haunts the glowing mind,
Limping Decorum lingers far behind;
Vainly the dotard mends her prudish pace,
Outstript and vanquish'd in the mental chase.

Then, Byron bursts out in opposition to the received wisdom. He will not tolerate the cant of middle-aged poets when he has such fresh blood coursing through his veins, such fire in his belly, such genius:

Oh! how I hate the nerveless, frigid song,
The ceaseless echo of the rhyming throng,
Whose labour'd lines, in chilling numbers flow,
To paint a pang the author ne'er can know!
('Answer to Some Elegant Verses')

It did not help Byron that his egotism ("I seek not glory from the senseless crowd") in the above poem contradicted what he said in the Preface to the collection: "I should be loth to ... triumph in honours granted solely to a title." Lord Henry Brougham, who reviewed Byron's book with what Jerome J. McGann has called "delightfully urbane acidity" (*Fiery Dust*, 4), was actually as sarcastic as one would expect an anonymous reviewer to be, 'thanking' Byron for condescending to participate in the bourgeois grubbiness of Grub Street business. When he first saw the review, Byron was "in such a rage as [he] ha[d] never been in since" and drunk three bottles of claret (in vain) to calm down (*Medwin's Conversations of Lord Byron*, 142). Yet it is worth reflecting on the gathering greatness of the 18-year-old poet, who, though clearly immersed in the work of Pope and others, was capable of declaring himself:

Untaught by worldly wisdom how to feign,
And check each impulse with prudential reign
('Childish Recollections', lines 59-60)

and confident in formulating his opposition to the way the world of men works:

When, all we feel, our honest souls disclose,
In love to friends, in open hate to foes;

No varnish'd tales the lips of youth repeat,
No dear-bought knowledge purchas'd by deceit;
Hypocrisy, the gift of lengthened years,
Matur'd by age, the garb of Prudence wears:
When, now, the Boy is ripen'd into Man,
His careful Sire chalks forth some wary plan;
Instructs his Son from Candour's path to shrink,
Smoothly to speak, and cautiously to think;
Still to assent, and never to deny –
A patron's praise can well reward the lie:
And who, when Fortune's warning voice is heard,
Would lose his opening prospects for a word?
Although, against that word, his heart rebel,
And Truth, indignant, all his bosom swell.
('Childish Recollections', lines 61-76)

Byron thought Francis Jeffrey (1773-1850), editor of the *Edinburgh Review* (1803-29), was the reviewer of *Hours of Idleness*. The poet wanted his revenge to be swift and preferably terminal, so he wrote *English Bards and Scotch Reviewers*, which is a petulant clearing of the throat indeed by the poet who would later produce *Childe Harold's Pilgrimage* and *Don Juan*:

Behold! in various throngs the scribbling crew,
For notice eager, pass in long review:
Each spurs his jaded Pegasus apace,
And Rhyme and Blank maintain an equal race;
Sonnets on sonnets crowd and ode on ode;
And Tales of Terror jostle on the road;
Immeasurable measures move along;
For simpering Folly loves a varied song ...

(143-150)

Again, Pope's *Essay on Criticism* comes to mind, where:

... tuneful fools ...
... haunt Parnassus but to please their ear,
Not mend their minds; as some to church repair,
Not for the doctrine, but the music there.

(2)

Clear is the vestigial adolescence in Byron's adjective-loaded salvoes. He attacks many writers. But his attacks are ineffectual, and his personality is "terribly wasted", as Wilde said, "in its battle with … stupidity, and hypocrisy, and Philistinism". Wordsworth is described as "simple" (237); Coleridge "brays" and is a "Laureate of the long-eared kind" (264); and Southey has "chaunt[ed] too often and too long" (225). Then Byron wrongly identifies the most obnoxious reviewer in the universe:

> Health to immortal JEFFREY! once, in name,
> England could boast a judge almost the same;
> In soul so like, so merciful, yet just,
> Some think that Satan has resigned his trust,
> And given the Spirit to the world again,
> To sentence Letters, as he sentenced men.
> With hand less mighty, but with heart as black,
> With voices as willing to decree the rack …
>
> (438-445)

The poem was published anonymously in March 1809, and Byron was very cautious about putting his name to a second edition. He quickly became embarrassed about it and "wished to cancel" many things about it, but as "[t]he thing was known to be [his], and [he] could not have escaped [his] enemies in not owning it", he did the "more manly" thing, and, "contrary to the advice of friends, [he] affixed [his] name." (*Medwin*, 144) It would not have been particularly worrying for a writer to be attacked in *English Bards*. The poem was the result of Byron's immature paranoia that had yet to evolve into the species of satire capable of hunting out and branding what is morally wrong (disguised as what is morally right).

In his essay, 'Byron and the Satiric Temper', P.M. Yarker follows the vengeful author of *English Bards* running at his targets with his sword unsheathed, but becoming sidetracked before reaching those targets, and becoming, as Hamlet would have put it, "unpregnant of [his] cause" (*Hamlet*, Act II, scene ii):

> Discursive, over-emphatic, always expanding and elaborating,
> [*English Bards*] suggests the opposite of the cold malice that

calculates the exact force and timing to produce the greatest
hurt.

(Byron: A Symposium, 82)

Of the many poets that Byron targeted in *English Bards*, only
Wordsworth could not forgive him. It was as if Byron's contemporaries knew and at some level sympathised with the promising
writer's hunger for recognition:

> Thus far I've held my undisturbed career,
> Prepared for rancour, steeled 'gainst selfish fear;
> This thing of rhyme I ne'er disdained to own –
> Though not obtrusive, yet not quite unknown:
> My voice was heard again, though not so loud,
> My page, though nameless, never disavowed;
> And now at once I tear the veil away: –
> Cheer on the pack! the Quarry stands at bay ...
>
> (1037-1043)

As Yarker says, "Byron seems too amused and excited by the poem
to consider its effect on its victims, whom he had no real wish to
harm." Consideration of *Hamlet* is germane here. Hamlet too had
wondered at the spectacle of himself prevaricating when he had in
fact revenge still to wreak:

> Why, what an ass am I! This is most brave,
> That I, the son of a dear father murdered,
> Prompted to my revenge by heaven and hell,
> Must like a whore unpack my heart with words ...
>
> (*Hamlet*, Act II, scene ii)

Speaking daggers but using none, Byron spins out a sense of his
own harmlessness that has an affinity with Hamlet's:

> The time hath been, when no harsh sound would fall
> From lips that now may seem imbued with gall;
> Nor fools nor follies tempt me to despise
> The meanest thing that crawled beneath my eyes:
> But now, so callous grown, so changed since youth,
> I've learned to think, and sternly speak the truth;

Learned to deride the critic's starch decree,
And break him on the wheel he meant for me ...

(1053-1060)

Byron's allusion to Pope's 'Epistle to Dr Arbuthnot' ("Satire or Sense, alas! can *Sporus* feel?/Who breaks a butterfly upon a wheel?") reveals that he is taking cognisance of his own career through the palimpsest of literary texts. It is the combination of wit and erudition that makes the expression of Byron's gall worth reading. For example, when Byron asked his nominal guardian, the Earl of Carlisle, to present him in the House of Lords, Carlisle replied unhelpfully, directing Byron vaguely in the direction of the appropriate paperwork. Byron retaliated by erasing the complimentary lines he had written about Carlisle, and inserting the following:

No Muse will cheer, with renovating smile,
The paralytic puling of CARLISLE.
The puny schoolboy and his early lay
Men pardon, if his follies pass away;
But who forgives the Senior's ceaseless verse,
Whose hairs grow hoary as his rhymes grow worse?

(725-730)

Having alluded to Carlisle's nervous disorder ("paralytic puling"), Byron sarcastically summarised Carlisle's accomplishments:

What heterogeneous honours deck the Peer!
Lord, rhymester, petit-maître, pamphleteer!

(731-732)

This is a crass jibe, and Byron would write in 1816 that Carlisle's "provocation was not sufficient to justify such acerbity." However, Byron was being visited by writer's remorse, not moral scruples: in *English Bards*, he had failed as a satirist because he picked up missiles too indiscriminately, and hurled them too artlessly, at the objects of his ire. By the time he came to write *Don Juan*, he had honed his facility for satire like a precision mechanism. Like the operator of a modern guillotine, the author of *Don Juan* would heave and release his gleaming versification with detachment and efficiency. To give one example, consider at the chilling tidiness with which the author of *Don Juan* dispatches even the spectral Keats:

> John Keats, who was killed off by one critique,
> Just as he really promised something great,
> If not intelligible, – without Greek
> Contrived to talk about the gods of late,
> Much as they might have been supposed to speak.
> Poor fellow! His was an untoward fate. –
> 'Tis strange the mind, that very fiery particle,
> Should let itself be snuffed out by an article.
>
> (*Don Juan*, XI, 60)

Meantime, however, in *Childe Harold*, the sheer wealth and vigour of Byron's sense of the things that happen to him resembles Hamlet's, in that the variety and the lack of an exact type of causal logic for every detail are part of the point.

4

Major Works

Childe Harold's Pilgrimage

Byron used the traditional Spenserian stanza, which he said he picked up from the Scottish poet, James Beattie (1735-1803). Here is a sample from Beattie's *The Minstrel; or, The Progress of Genius*, Book I (1771):

> In truth he was a strange and wayward wight,
> Fond of each gentle and each dreadful scene.
> In darkness and in storm he found delight:
> Nor less, than when on ocean-wave serene
> The southern sun diffused his dazzling sheen.
> Even sad vicissitude amused his soul:
> And if a sight would sometimes intervene,
> And down his cheek a tear of pity roll,
> A sigh, a tear so sweet, he wished not to control.

Here is a sample from Byron's *Childe Harold's Pilgrimage*, Canto 16:

> Self-exiled Harold wanders forth again,
> With naught of Hope left – but with less of gloom;
> The very knowledge that he lived in vain,
> That all was over on this side the tomb,
> Had made Despair a smilingness assume,
> Which, though 'twere wild, – as on the plundered wreck
> When mariners would madly meet their doom
> With draughts intemperate on the sinking deck, –
> Did yet inspire a cheer, which he forbore to check.

Childe Harold's Pilgrimage, though influenced by much of the same melancholy material as influenced Wordsworth's poetry, was originally intended by Byron to be full of humour. But it is not very humorous. The style seems not to allow the poet to do what he is really naturally good at. *Don Juan* would later allow him to give full vent to his force as a poet. The achievement of *Childe Harold* is that it gives the sense of travelogue (in which everything ordinary is made to seem extraordinary), and the sense of melancholy:

> There is a very life in our despair,
> Vitality of poison, – a quick root
> Which feeds these deadly branches; for it were
> As nothing did we die; but Life will suit
> Itself to Sorrow's most detested fruit,
> Like to the apples on the Dead Sea's shore,
> All ashes to the taste ...
>
> (III, 34)

Byron is adept at bringing ego into the narrative. For all his opposition to Wordsworth's "simple" poetry, Byron must have spent much time immersed in it:

> I live not in myself, but I become
> Portion of that around me; and to me
> High mountains are a feeling, but the hum
> Of human cities torture ...
>
> (III, 72)

One thinks of Wordsworth's 'Lines composed a few miles above Tintern Abbey, on revisiting the banks of the Wye' (1798), in which the colours and the forms of the Lake District's mountainous scenery "were then to [Wordsworth]/An appetite", whereas he found the city "joyless" and "unprofitable".

Byron adds to this the feeling in the reader that the protagonist is interesting and mysterious. When the narrator of *Childe Harold's Pilgrimage* asks "What deep wounds ever closed without a scar?" (III, 84) the reader is intrigued by the autobiographical possibilities. (In spite of Byron's letter to R.C. Dallas, dated 31st October 1811, which claimed: "I by no means intend to identify myself with *Harold*, but ... *deny* all connection with him ... I would not be such a fellow as I have made my hero for all the world.") After all, a few stanzas earlier, Byron mentioned the first confessional autobiographer (in the modern sense), Jean-Jacques Rousseau (1712-1778):

> The apostle of Affliction, he who threw
> Enchantment over Passion, and from Woe
> Wrung overwhelming eloquence ...
> ... yet he knew
> How to make Madness beautiful, and cast
> O'er erring deeds and thoughts, a heavenly hue
> Of words ...
>
> (III, 77)

The reader will of course wonder exactly what "Madness" Byron has made beautiful, and may look to the newspapers for a prosaic explanation. Byron's loyal friend, John Cam Hobhouse, wrote in his diary:

> the great success of 'Childe Harold' is due chiefly to Byron's having dared to give utterance to certain feelings which every one must have encouraged in the melancholy and therefore morbid hours of his existence ...

In his dedication to Canto IV, Byron confesses to the reader for the first time that:

> there will be found less of the pilgrim than in any of the preceding, and ... little slightly, if at all, separated from the author speaking in his own person. The fact is, that I had become weary of drawing a line which every one seemed determined not to perceive.

Byron forfeits the disguise, claiming that he prefers (insouciantly) to defer to the majority of his readership's perception. In saying this, he jettisons the burden of having to constantly posture for his public. His public is now helping him substantially to retain and renew his attractive blend of beauty, pedigree, sexual magnetism (and ambivalence), and doom. In his later romances, Byron's characters will all be similarly mysterious, yet autobiographically interpretable, with their Gothic secrets. The protagonists in Byron's dramas will be like forces of the appetites, acting darkly and savagely rather than like human beings.

Byron can make readers understand him at once. To read the beginning of Canto IV of *Childe Harold's Pilgrimage* is to view, as it were, the theatre of one's mind being lit up to its lavish potential:

> I stood in Venice, on the Bridge of Sighs,
> A palace and a prison on each hand:
> I saw from out the wave her structures rise
> As from the stroke of the Enchanter's wand ...

Byron's imagination unites a diction so magnificently ordered that it lulls the senses, like an intoxicating melody, stirring the soul of the sensitive reader. So ingenious, so masterly is the poet's choice of words that none could with justice be robbed of its right to be there. One feels that Byron has opened up a wide perspective that sets one dreaming of its meaning, at once precise and manifold. One feels as Proust (that epicure of similarly delicious reveries) felt on reading magical literature:

> How often, in the *Divine Comedy*, in Shakespeare, I have had this impression of having in front of me, inserted into the present moment, something of the past, that dream-like impression one feels in Venice, on the Piazzetta, before its two columns of pink and grey granite which carry on their capitals, the one the lion of St Mark and the other St Theodore trampling on the crocodile – beautiful foreigners come there from the Orient across the sea they are gazing at in the distance and which comes to die at their feet ...
> ('On Reading', 1906)

Dante, Shakespeare, Byron and Proust could all conceive and condense the expressions of their ideas into work that would become a communion, an interchange of thought between magic-working author and ideal reader, a mental collaboration by consent between scattered persons. But Byron's power to conjure, say, that exquisite picture of Venice becomes powerless in the mind of a less imaginative reader. The critic, Samuel Rogers, used the above lines as an illustration of Byron's carelessness:

There is a great deal of incorrect and hasty writing in Byron's works; but it is overlooked in this age of hasty readers. For instance,

> I stood in Venice, on the Bridge of Sighs,
> A palace and a prison *on each hand.*

He meant to say, that on one hand was a palace, on the other a prison …
(*Recollections of the Table Talk of Samuel Rogers*, 244)

In those moments when he experienced the anxieties of the nervous practitioner of poetry, Byron himself would have agreed (in private) with Rogers's view (as he did to Thomas Moore when, having published *The Corsair*, he worried about his "own want of judgement …"). But Byron was nevertheless driven to write the way he did, feeling in his heart that there was something *else* in his writing, something infinitely more original, significant and rigorous than the mere readability and textual thinness perceived by unkind critics. Rogers – like many first-class, but pedantic, lovers of the English language – feels something like a physical pain on reading the beginning of *Childe Harold*, Canto IV, which has offended him deeply and made him angry. Rogers professes his concern with the question of something meaning what it means, and not meaning something else. Rogers's point is, if you really understand the English language, Byron's sentence about the palace and the prison is not saying what Byron thinks it is saying, and the sad thing is that it means to many readers what the writer erroneously thinks it means. Rogers is foreshadowing the reservations of some of the Victorian critics about Byron's writing. George Eliot (1819-80) would, later, call Byron "a vulgar genius". Later still, T.S. Eliot, writing in 1937, would feel sufficiently emboldened to say that:

> The bulk of Byron's verse is distressing in proportion to its quality … We have come to expect poetry to be something very concentrated, something distilled; but if Byron had distilled his verse, there would have been nothing whatever left.

That utterance, from such a hugely influential critic as T.S. Eliot, is a pristine illustration of what Ezra Pound (1885-1972), in his poem

'Commission', called "the tyranny of the unimaginative". That un-imaginative reaction to Byron's work has been spread so thoroughly through the reading public (up to this day) that even Rupert Christiansen can say "It is no use considering Byron now as a serious poet." (Christiansen, 198) One thinks of the timelessness of Pope's insight, and the necessity of becoming reacquainted with it:

> Whoever thinks a faultless piece to see,
> Thinks what ne'er was, nor is, nor e'er shall be ...
> And if the means be just, the conduct true,
> Applause, in spite of trivial faults, is due ...
> Most critics, fond of some subservient art,
> Still make the Whole depend upon a Part:
> They talk of principles ...
>
> (*An Essay on Criticism*, II)

When we read for ourselves the opening lines of *Childe Harold*, Canto IV, we *do* know (of course we do!) what Byron means to mean. We accept, in imagination, the elegant symmetry of the opening image. Exultant at the prospect of the poet continuing to share with us his imaginative riches, we are no more interested in carping at the wobbly grammar than we are in seeing the beautifully crumbling Venice (or the raven-inhabited Newstead Abbey, which Byron inherited at the age of ten) refurbished. There is a special understanding between Byron and the reader: in *Byron and the Spoiler's Art* (1960), Paul West has recognised Byron's "loose assumption of our sympathy." (60) Byron is, like us all, in the gutter. The maw of his conscience contains half-remembered sins, and sexually-degenerate urges. He is like Shakespeare's quintessence of all men, Hamlet:

> I am myself indifferent honest, but yet I could accuse me of such things that it were better my mother had not borne me. I am very proud, revengeful, ambitious, with more offences at my beck than I have thoughts to put them in, imagination to give them shape, or time to act them in. What should such fellows as I do crawling between earth and heaven? We are arrant knaves all. Believe none of us.
>
> (*Hamlet*, Act III, scene i)

Yes, Byron does – like that elect "some of us" eulogised whimsically by Wilde – look at the stars from time to time, but that does not change the reality that *he is, like all men, in the gutter.*

While it conveys clearly that he has availed of his privilege as an aristocrat and read his Gibbon (*The History of the Decline and Fall of the Roman Empire* [1776-88]) – for example:

> The Suabian sued, and now the Austrian reigns –
> An Emperor tramples where an Emperor knelt;
> Kingdoms are shrunk to provinces, and chains
> Clank over sceptred cities; Nations melt
> From Power's high pinnacle, when they have felt
> The sunshine for a while, and downward go
> Like Lauwine loosened from the mountain's belt;
> Oh for one hour of blind old Dandolo!
> Th'octogenarian chief, Byzantium's conquering foe
>
> (IV, 12)

Byron's idiom is – like his public image – saleably 'dishevelled', as if it/he has just emerged from the rubble caused by his last violent showdown with the Establishment (or the demons in himself). Hence, the consistently 'faulty' poetry of the *Flawed Angel* (as Grosskurth calls Byron), with, as Walter Scott noticed, its "solecisms" and "singularities" (*Quarterly Review*, XIX, 1818); or, as Algernon Charles Swinburne (1837-1909) would call them, the "blundering, floundering, lumbering and stumbling stanzas", the "gasping, ranting, wheezing, broken-winded verse". But while Swinburne would hear in *Childe Harold* the "alternate moan and bellow from the trampled platform of theatrical misanthropy", he would simultaneously "discern in the thick and troubled stream of [Byron's] natural eloquence whatever of value may be swept along in company with such drifting rubbish." (*Miscellanies*, 1886, 74-6). One can just envisage the muttonchops astride the mouth from whence that faint praise came.

Most influentially, Thomas Carlyle (1795-1881) wrote his indictment of Byron's unbelief in *Sartor Resartus* (1833-34), his spiritual autobiography:

> I asked myself: What is this that, ever since earliest years,
> thou hast been fretting and fuming, and lamenting and self-

tormenting, on account of? Say it in a word: it is not because thou art not HAPPY? Because the THOU (sweet gentleman) is no sufficiently honoured, nourished, soft-bedded, and lovingly cared-for? Foolish soul! A little while ago thou hadst no right to *be* at all. What if thou wert born and predestined not to be Happy, but to be Unhappy! Art thou nothing other than a Vulture, then, that fliest through the Universe seeking after somewhat to *eat*; and shrieking dolefully because carrion enough is not given thee? Close thy *Byron*; open thy *Goethe*.

The above passage is surely the record of Carlyle attacking something in himself that Byron's poetry had actually enabled him to identify. It is as if Carlyle has seen in Byron's work the too-vivid apparition of his naked sorrows, and wants to flee to the work of Goethe who, although he had invented the suicidal Romantic outsider in his novella, *Die Leiden des Jungen Werthers* (1774), refused afterwards to indulge again the negative emotions that made the writing of that book necessary. Goethe would call his life "the perpetual rolling of a rock that must be raised up again forever" (quoted in Colin Wilson's *The Outsider* [1956]). That idea of the joyless effort of existing has somehow seemed preferable to the idea of having fun in the verbal playground. Joyless existence has been justified intellectually by existentialism. The twentieth- or twenty-first-century writer is expected to be an existentialist, or a feminist, or a Marxist, or a postmodernist, or some other -ist. And those writers who died before such -isms were born have since had their work re-interpreted; hence, the work of Laurence Sterne has been delivered to first-time readers along the lines of Russian formalism, and Milton has acquired the interpretive dimensions of Marxism and feminism (*Practising Theory and Reading Literature* [ed. Raman Selden], 1989). Because Byron did not really fit with the great law, as the poet, James Reeves, defined it, "that a writer must be 'committed' [in some ideological way, or to some political cause]", his poetry has not been taken as seriously as it should be. Reeves' eloquent reaction against the mass conformity that suffocates the voice of the individual poet is worth quoting (with Byron in mind):

A poet is first a man, and as a man he is committed, whether he likes it or not, to an attitude, if not to action, in respect of the public events of his time. But that his attitude towards these must somehow be made to engage his sensibility as a poet is not so certain. To me poetry is rooted in the particular and the immediate. How therefore can I write poetry about what is experienced mainly through the newspapers, the films, and the radio? If any can make poems out of this, I can only admire and do otherwise. It may be that this is an unpoetic time. The nightmare of sensationalism, violence, hysteria and threatened destruction which presses in on us as we read the news removes all relevance and meaning from the only kind of poetry I can write. If a poet has a function today, it is to assert his individuality in the midst of all the pressures towards conformity to some pattern of group thinking and feeling. 'Know yourself' is perhaps the only useful advice which can be given to a poet; and 'Be yourself' is the only message a poet can give to anyone else.

Even though Byron has very serious things to say, critics equipped to discuss modern literary theories have too often, at best, limited enthusiasm for his individual stylistic exuberance. The more words spent in an essay admiring the artistry, the less words will be available to help gather the text convincingly into a pigeon-hole.

One would do better to avoid the wasteful activity of much literary criticism, and benefit instead from Byron's poetry's power and refinement, which still gives off new savours, new intoxications:

> But unto us she [Venice] hath a spell beyond
> Her name in story, and her long array
> Of mighty shadows, whose dim forms despond
> Above the Dogeless city's vanished sway:
> Ours is a trophy which will not decay
> With the Rialto; Shylock and the Moor,
> And Pierre cannot be swept or worn away –
> The keystones of the arch! though all were o'er,
> For us repeopled were the solitary shore.
>
> (IV, 4)

> … by these Spirits supplied,
> First exiles, then replaces what we hate;
> Watering the heart whose early flowers have died,
> And with a fresher growth, replenishing the void.
>
> (IV, 5)

The above lines speak to us directly, and simply, about what Venice means to Byron, and to us, as readers of literature. We are made complicit in the poet's sense of wonder (at the shared riches in the mental commonwealth) in a way that has been routinely rejected by sophisticated theorists:

> The assaults made by modern conditions upon the individ-
> uality, or what may be called the privacy, of an intelligent and
> sensitive person are considerable – more so than perhaps we
> realise. It is becoming increasingly difficult to 'get on with
> one's own life'. It seems to me that some of the younger poets
> (and perhaps the best of them) have been shocked [in the mid-
> twentieth-century] into a kind of defensive sophistication, an
> attitude in which contemporary critical doctrine needs to
> confirm them. If poetry dies of over-sophistication, it will not
> be the first time. To be afraid to express feeling may result in
> an inhibition of feeling itself.
>
> (James Reeves, Introduction to *Collected Poems:*
> *1929-1959* [1960].)

Contemporary readers were attuned to Byron's poetry in the same way that devotees of pop and rock music would be attuned to their icons' utterances. (In the 1960s, ageing musicologists would not reverse many enthusiasts' passion for the songs of Lennon and McCartney.) There is the feeling in Byron's work that all the effort has been made by the writer for the reader, and that s/he does not have to retrace too many steps taken superfluously in pursuit of misunderstood metaphors. All is bright and clear to view – the sight of Venice, and the narrator's sense of that city's history, are dropped into the reader's mind with something akin to slick stagecraft:

> A thousand Years their cloudy wings expand
> Around me, and a dying Glory smiles
> O'er the far times, when many a subject land
> Looked to the winged Lion's marble piles,
> Where Venice sate in state, throned on her hundred isles!
>
> (IV, 1)

Shelley's poetry is much more difficult to understand, and it is no surprise that at the time Shelley's works sold very poorly in comparison with Byron's. Francis Thompson's beautiful essay on

Shelley explains that the poet "stood ... at the very junction-lines of the visible and invisible, and could shift the points as he willed", and that "He could express as he listed the material and the immaterial in terms of each other." But the reader has to work to attune himself to Shelley's use of imagery, to adapt himself to Shelley's world. In the Preface to *Prometheus Unbound* (1820), Shelley does recognise the difficulty:

> The imagery which I have employed will be found, in many instances, to have been drawn from the operations of the human mind, or from those external actions by which they are expressed. This is unusual in modern poetry, although Dante and Shakespeare are full of instances of the same kind.

In Shelley's vision, imagery and symbolism are closely akin. Throughout Shelley's work, the same caves, islands, journeys, moonlight, and starlight recur. They are all associated with the acquisition of wisdom, but the poet does not explain the pattern. He seems, rather, to expect the reader to recognise that they are in fact traditional symbols in the literature of quest. Shelley's interest in metaphysics came from his interest in the ideas of Plato, who had argued that the temporal world is a poor imitation of the real world of perfect, eternal forms. Plato thought that men could know something of eternal reality through contemplation. Shelley's work, therefore, was really part of the esoteric tradition which, though it is the driving force behind all that he (and William Blake before him) wrote, made him seem obscure to the uninitiated reader when he said things like "Poets are the hierophants of an unapprehended inspiration: the mirrors of the gigantic shadows which futurity casts upon the present ..." ('A Defence of Poetry'.)

There was no system of poetry, or philosophy, with which readers had to be au fait before they could consider themselves serious readers of Byron. There was no higher pressure of thinking which readers needed to attain in order to be able to assimilate Byron's concepts and insights. *Childe Harold* can be read, or rather, consumed, as passively as any undemanding novel. "He simply discovered that he could do it, do it fast ... and that people bought the results." (Chritiansen, 198) Byron did concede in one stanza of *Childe Harold* that "The Beings of the Mind are not of clay", and that,

Essentially immortal, they create
And multiply in us a brighter ray
And more beloved existence: that which Fate
Prohibits to dull life in this our state
Of mortal bondage ...

(IV, 5)

But in the next stanza he asserted the even greater luminosity of facts, or, as Seamus Perry says in his essay, 'The Romantic Matter of Fact', "their *factuality*: namely, the sheer, intransigent, unique *givenness* of them." Perry continues: "To welcome [facts] promises to undermine the idealist's most basic claim, that all experience is made and not given ..." Byron welcomes facts: "Yet there are things whose strong reality/Outshines our fairy-land" (*Childe Harold*, IV, vi). When he describes "meek Dian's crest" "Float[ing] through the azure air – an island of the blest!", he feels the need to include a footnote asserting the veracity of the image: "The above description may seem fantastical or exaggerated to those who have never seen an Oriental or an Italian sky; yet it is ... literal ..." Byron, as always keen to maintain his strong grasp on the actual, asserts that he has actually seen what he describes. He wrote elsewhere that "the grand object of life is sensation – to feel that we exist – even though in pain" (*Letters and Journals*, III, 109). In that case, how are we to feel when, two stanzas later, he conveys the sense of transition from day to night by describing the various stages of the death of a dolphin?

... a paler Shadow strews
Its mantle o'er the mountains; parting Day
Dies like the Dolphin, whom each pang imbues
With a new colour as it gasps away –
The last still loveliest, till – 'tis gone – and all is gray.

(IV, 29)

Did Byron once stand idly by, watching the final struggle of a washed-up dolphin? The image is intriguing and unsettling, as if something vaguely like a scalp has been offered to us by someone we suspect of inhumanity. One thinks of the moment in Schopenhauer's essay, 'The Christian System', where Schopenhauer expresses his disgust at the inhumanity behind Jung Stilling's writing:

It is a revolting thing that a writer who is so pious and Christian in his sentiments as Jung Stilling should use a simile like this, in his *Scenen aus dem Geisterreich* (bk. II, sc. I, p.15). "Suddenly the skeleton shrivelled up into an indescribably hideous and dwarf-like form, just as when you bring a large spider into the focus of a burning glass, and watch the purulent blood hiss and bubble in the heat." This man of God then was guilty of such infamy or looked on quietly when another was committing it! in either case it comes to the same thing here. So little harm did he think of it that he tells us of it in passing, and without a trace of emotion.

(Religion: A Dialogue, Demopheles–Philalethes And Other Essays, trans. T. Bailey Sanders)

Unhampered by the exigencies of maintaining a pious reputation, Byron traces the roots of these flourishing moral ambivalences down into the personal darkness that nourishes them. He says, in one stanza, that "alone ... man with his God must strive" (IV, xxxiii), but in the next stanza he balances his overall view of the heavenly and hellish sources of human creativity:

> Or, it may be, with Demons, who impair
> The strength of better thoughts, and seek their prey
> In melancholy bosoms – such as were
> Of moody texture from their earliest day,
> And loved to dwell in darkness and dismay,
> Deeming themselves predestined to a doom
> Which is not of the pangs that pass away;
> Making the Sun like blood, the Earth a tomb
> The tomb a hell – and Hell itself a murkier gloom.

(IV, 34)

The Byronic vision was easily translatable, so Byron had a European audience. (The radiance of many Wordsworthian and Shelleyan metaphors would be more easily lost in translation.) The common reader could quickly comprehend Byron's poetry, so not only was there a huge difference between Byron's and ("the perceived vulgar, plebeian") Keats' readerships; there was also a huge difference between Byron's and (the aristocratic) Shelley's readerships:

Byron believed that the Cockneys, the Lakers, indeed all the 'new Schools' were at one in wrong-headedly trying to reform English poetry by following a "system." Their deliberate rejection of Pope's cultural and aesthetic environment mattered more to Byron than the differences between Oxbridge-educated poets committed to life in the English countryside and petty bourgeois Londoners whose poetry openly celebrated the pleasures of an outing on Hampstead Heath.

('Byron Reads Keats', by William C. Keach)

During his creative labours, Byron often found his imagination wandering off amidst the old tangles of Wordsworthian/Coleridgean thought:

> I live not in myself, but I become
> Portion of that around me; and to me
> High mountains are a feeling, but the hum
> Of human cities torture: I can see
> Nothing to loathe in Nature, save to be
> A link reluctant in a fleshly chain,
> Classed among creatures, when the soul can flee,
> And with the sky – the peak – the heaving plain
> Of ocean, or the stars, mingle – and not in vain.
>
> (III, 72)

In this particular instance, Byron allows his imagination a prolonged wander (lasting four Spenserian stanzas), before demanding it back to meditate amongst decay:

> And thus I am absorbed ...
>
> (III, 73)

> Are not the mountains, waves, and skies a part
> Of me and of my Soul, as I of them?
> Is not the love of these deep in my heart
> With a pure passion? should I not contemn
> All objects, if compared with these? and stem
> A tide of suffering ...
>
> (III, 75)

But this is not my theme; and I return
To that which is immediate ...

(III, 76)

Byron raps himself on the knuckles and gets back, as it were, to his
castle, where his crown jewels sit side by side with Pope's, and are
not to be taken away by those levelling Cockneys or Lakers.

In his novel, *Nightmare Abbey* (1818), Thomas Love Peacock
satirised Byron ("Mr. Cypress") not just as the bad husband –

> *Mr. Cypress.* – Sir, I have quarrelled with my wife; and a man
> who has quarrelled with his wife is absolved from all duty to
> his country. I have written an ode to tell the people as much,
> and they may take it as they list

– but also as one of England's proponents of strenuous despair and
negativity:

> *Mr. Cypress.* – I have no hope for myself or for others. Our
> life is a false nature; it is not in the harmony of things; it is an
> all-blasting upas, whose root is earth, and whose leaves are
> the skies which rain their poison-dews upon mankind. We
> wither from our youth; we gasp with unslaked thirst for
> unattainable good; lured from the first to the last by phantoms
> – love, fame, ambition, avarice – all idle, and all ill – one
> meteor of many names, that vanishes in the smoke of death.
>
> (Chapter XI)

In the above passages, "Mr. Cypress" is about to leave England (as
Byron did in 1816). Compare the passage just above with the
following stanzas from Byron himself:

> We wither from our youth, we gasp away –
> Sick – sick; unfound the boon – unslaked the thirst,
> Though to the last, in verge of our decay,
> Some phantom lures, such as we sought at first –
> But all too late,– so are we doubly curst.
> Love, Fame, Ambition, Avarice – 'tis the same,
> Each idle – and all ill – and none the worst –
> For all are meteors with a different name,
> And Death the sable smoke where vanishes the flame.
>
> (*Childe Harold*, IV, 124)

Our life is a false nature – 'tis not in
The harmony of things, – this hard decree,
This uneradicable taint of Sin,
This boundless Upas, this all-blasting tree,
Whose root is Earth – whose leaves and branches be
The skies which rain their plagues on men like dew –
Disease, death, bondage – all the woes we see,
And worse, the woes we see not – which throb through
The immedicable soul, with heart-aches ever new.

(Childe Harold, IV, 126)

Peacock parodies Byron, as he parodies Coleridge ("Mr. Flosky")
and Shelley ("Scythrop"), in a way that reveals his understanding
admiration as much as his flair for satiric pastiche:

> *Mr. Cypress.* – Human love! Love is not an inhabitant of the
> earth. We worship him as the Athenians did their unknown
> God: but broken hearts are the martyrs of his faith, and the
> eye shall never see the form which phantasy paints, and which
> passion pursues through paths of delusive beauty, among
> flowers whose odors are agonies, and tree whose gums are
> poison.

One thinks of J.K. Huysmans' (1848-1907) tribute to Charles
Baudelaire (1821-1867):

> But Baudelaire had gone further; he had descended to the
> bottom of the inexhaustible mine, had pushed his way along
> abandoned or unexplored galleries, had penetrated those
> districts of the soul where the monstrous vegetations of the
> sick mind flourish.
>
> *(A Rebours* [1884], Chapter 12)

Huysmans was not joking when he wrote the above about Baudelaire.
Similarly, Peacock's tributes to Byron, whether they are expressed
in prose or in poetry, are, despite being parts of a satire, shot through
with genuine admiration for the poet's genius:

> *Mr. Cypress.* – The mind is diseased of its own beauty, and
> fevers into false creation. The forms which the sculptor's soul
> has seized exist only in himself

and

> Mr. Cypress sung –
> There is a fever of the spirit,
> The brand of Cain's unresting doom,
> Which in the lone dark souls that bear it
> Glows like the lamp in Tullia's tomb:
> Unlike that lamp, its subtle fire
> Burns, blasts, consumes its cell, the heart,
> Till, one by one, hope, joy, desire,
> Like dreams of shadowy smoke depart.
> When hope, love, life itself, are only
> Dust – spectral memories – dead and cold –
> The unfed fire burns bright and lonely,
> Like that undying lamp of old:
> And by that drear illumination,
> Till time its clay-built home has rent,
> Thought broods on feeling's desolation –
> The soul is its own monument.

The Giaour (A Turkish Tale)

> Stick to the East; – the oracle, [Madame de] Staël, told me it
> was the only poetical policy. The North, South and West, have
> all been exhausted; but from the East, we have nothing but
> Southey's unsaleables … the public are orientalising.
>
> (quoted by Christiansen, 195)

Byron took the advice. *The Giaour* (1813) was his first Oriental tale, and it was even more popular than *Childe Harold*. It is a long narrative poem that, as Byron stated in the Advertisement, was presented in "disjointed fragments". His memories of his travels were in him impatiently awaiting articulation, so the delivery became like a phased exorcism of exoticism. Byron told Thomas Moore in 1821 that "if I don't write to empty my mind, I go mad … I feel it as a torture, which I must get rid of, but never as a pleasure" (*Letters and Journals*, VIII, 55). In his essay, 'Wordsworth Writing', Andrew Bennett effectively concurs with Martin Seymour-Smith (in his essay on Wordsworth in *Poets Through Their Letters*, 312-313): "for Wordsworth the act of writing was itself associated with bad eyes, headaches, bowel complaints, chest pains, irritability, fatigue, insomnia" (*The Wordsworth Circle*, vol. XXXIV, no. 1, Winter 2003, 3). Byron shares with Wordsworth joylessness in the compositional process. Caroline Franklin notes that "The first MS draft had been 406 lines and the first published edition 685, but by the seventh the poem had swelled to 1334 lines." (*Byron: A Literary Life*, 51). Byron told Murray that *The Giaour* was "a snake of a poem" and said that it had been "lengthening its rattles every month" (*Letters and Journals*, III, 100). The notion of Byron's heterogeneous "dark-bright" (MacCarthy, 183) memories emerging in that way is simultaneously alluring and grotesque: on the one hand, one thinks of the turbaned poet charming the ever-lengthening "snake" from its basket, white minarets and mosque glittering in the background; on the other hand, one thinks of the agonised poet in the throes of delivering something unaccountably long and reptilian. Whichever of those two interpretations is closer to what Byron had in mind, they both suggest something very important about the nature of creativity. Byron claimed that poetry "won't come when called". Such a claim suggests that poetry is a form of life, and that it does its own thing with or without the poet's leave: it will spread its wings (or lengthen its rattles) in a frightening way, or it will remain curled in the basket indefinitely, so that one would be tempted to suspect that it is not there at all. And still, Byron feels that it *is* there, and he feels that there is no frustration quite the equal of intuiting a coherence that refuses to emerge into the full daylight of objectifying comprehension. Byron's view on the subject of the poet's relationship to the muse has been influential:

> I have thought over most of my subjects for years before writing a line … You might as well ask me to describe an earth-quake whilst the ground was trembling under my feet.
> (Edward John Trelawny, *Records of Shelley, Byron and the Author*, 221)

Coleridge would preface his poem, *Kubla Khan*, with the claim that the images of the poem "rose up before him as *things* … without any sensation or consciousness of effort." How interesting it is that Coleridge published *Kubla Khan* in 1816 – that is, three years after the publication of *The Giaour* – with Byron's encouragement, and through Byron's publisher.

The story of *The Giaour* is based on a real event from Byron's travels in Turkey. He is supposed to have rescued at gunpoint a Turkish woman sewn up in a sack and about to be drowned by the Turks for adultery. Fiona MacCarthy does not let it escape her notice that there are two versions of that story. In the other version, the woman was already dead in the sack (MacCarthy, 132). At any rate, the story of *The Giaour* involves the adventure of Leila, a female slave who is freed from the harem of the Turkish warrior, Hassan, by her lover, a young Venetian known as the Giaour. Recaptured, Leila is thrown into the sea for infidelity. She is avenged by her lover.

The multiplicity of different narrative viewpoints in *The Giaour* has perplexed and divided academics. Byron's method seems messy. Did he mean to leave a problematic poem (in the same way that James Joyce [1882-1941] would knowingly leave *Finnegans Wake* [1939] behind for the attention of the PhD industry), or was it beyond (or beneath) his talents to make the necessary corrections and revisions? Franklin has leapt to Byron's defence:

> Some critics have assumed this method of composition to be the slipshod practice of a dilettante, too lazy to ensure coherence and unity. But it was rather that the poet was aiming at a daring experiment in abandoning his original straightforward plot. He was testing readers' reactions in assessing how far he could go in breaking down narrative into evocative fragments narrated from differing points of view for the reader to piece together.
>
> (*Byron: A Literary Life*, 51)

It may well be the case that the poet was experimenting with increasingly wanton narrative dislocation. Or it may be that he was "too lazy to ensure coherence and unity." (The obtuse reader may interpret the lacunae in Shelley's notebook poetry as evidence of Shelley's lack of sustained focus.)

The Giaour is like a box from which, when opened, Arabia breathes:

> And if at times a transient breeze
> Break the blue crystal of the seas,
> Or sweep one blossom from the trees,

How welcome is each gentle air
That wakes and wafts the odours there!

(16-20)

The melancholic Byron appeals to an audience amongst which there
are many women. He also appeals to the many men in that audience
with a discreet appetite for sensual reading experiences:

And grateful yields that smiling sky
Her fairest hue and fragrant sigh.
And many a summer flower is there,
And many a shade that Love might share,
And many a grotto, meant for rest,
That holds the pirate for a guest;
Whose bark in sheltering cove below
Lurks for the passing peaceful prow,
'Till the gay mariner's guitar
Is heard, and seen the Evening Star;
Then stealing with the muffled oar,
Far shaded by the rocky shore ...

(32-43)

Byron's Giaour moves through the exotic scenery:

Why looks he o'er the olive wood? –
The Crescent glimmers on the hill,
The Mosque's high lamps are quivering still ...

(221-223)

Giaour is an Arabic word meaning 'infidel' (or 'not Muslim'). The
Giaour is a citizen of no country, a believer in no god, and a servant
of no king. In other words, the Giaour is Byron. In his autobiography,
Seven Pillars of Wisdom (1926), T.E. Lawrence (1888-1935) would
silently allude to the Giaour, the general figure of the Byronic outcast:

In my case, the effort for these years to live in the dress of the
Arabs, and to imitate their mental foundation, quitted me of
my English self, and let me look at the West and its conventions
with new eyes: they destroyed it all for me. At the same time
I could not sincerely take on the Arab skin: it was an affectation
only. Easily was a man made an infidel, but hardly might he

be converted to another faith. I had dropped one form and not taken on the other, and was become like Mohammed's coffin in our legend, with a resultant feeling of intense loneliness in life, and a contempt, not for other men, but for all they do.

The exotic scenery is not necessarily the Giaour's provenance, but it is certainly Hassan's:

> 'Twas sweet of yore to see it [the stream] play
> And chase the sultriness of day –
> As springing high the silver dew
> In whirls fantastically flew,
> And flung luxurious coolness round
> The air, and verdure o'er the ground. –
> 'Twas sweet, when cloudless stars were bright,
> To view the wave of watery light,
> And hear its melody by night. –
> And oft had Hassan's childhood played
> Around the verge of that cascade;
> And oft upon his mother's breast
> That sound had harmonized his rest;
> And oft had Hassan's Youth along
> Its bank been soothed by Beauty's song ...
>
> (299-313)

A little later in the poem the reader is brought, as it were, to stand on the razor-thin bridge leading to the Muslim paradise:

> Though on Al-Sirat's arch I stood,
> Which totters o'er the fiery flood,
> With Paradise within my view,
> And all his Houris beckoning through ...
>
> (483-486)

Byron overflows with non-Christian images and concepts. Non-Christian himself, he does not feel obliged to comment critically on behalf of his Christian readership. He has simply packed the casket with eastern treasures for western readers to unlock for themselves. Other contemporary writers were more eager to flatter English readers as members of the superior race, and believers in the one, true God. At the core of De Quincey's *Confessions of an English Opium-Eater* there is a visceral hatred of all things eastern, and the *English* opium-eater is keen to distance himself from his Oriental counterparts:

> Under the connecting feeling of tropical heat and vertical sun-lights, I brought together [in opium dreams] all creatures, birds, beasts, reptiles, all trees and plants, usages and appearances, that are found in all tropical regions, and assembled them together in China or Indostan. From kindred feelings, I soon brought Egypt and all her gods under the same law. I was stared at, hooted at, grinned at, chattered at, by monkeys, by paroquets, by cockatoos. I ran into pagodas: and was fixed, for centuries, at the summit, or in secret rooms; I was the idol; I was the priest; I was worshipped; I was sacrificed ... I was buried, for a thousand years, in stone coffins, with mummies and sphinxes, in narrow chambers at the heart of eternal pyramids. Was kissed, with cancerous kisses, by crocodiles; and laid, confounded with all unutterable slimy things, amongst reeds and Nilotic mud.

De Quincey demonstrates his fear of becoming an Oriental (in taking opium), and of not doing any work at all. His opium-eater becomes an image for an alternative way of life that threatens 19th-century industrial European capitalism, so he ameliorates that threat by peppering his writing with references to the virtues of achievement, productivity and not wasting one's opportunities in life. De Quincey was very much part of his time in that he carefully informed his middle-class readers that the consumption of opium in a British, Christian (as opposed to an eastern, god-forsaken) spirit was possible.

Byron panders to no such prejudice because, as Bertrand Russell (1872-1970) put it, "he felt himself the equal of Satan" (*History of Western Thought*, 718). More mordantly than De Quincey, Byron feels the need to reaffirm the unpalatable truth delivered the previous century by Johnson: the vanity of all human wishes ("from China to Peru"). In Robert F. Gleckner's view:

> Byron's 'heroes' are no heroes in the ordinary sense; they are not participants in tragedy, yet they still retain some of the stature of the tragic hero. Like the tragic hero, they are man magnified, macrocosmic, titanic – yet nevertheless small, insignificant, and lost. They are not merely victims, nor are

they tyrants; they are a mixture of both, half dust, half deity, at war constantly. The loser, of course, is always self.

('*The Giaour* as Experimental Narrative')

The Giaour's alienation and his dark secret have brought him by degrees to his death; but so too have his better qualities (a particularly Byronic caveat). In short, whatever combination of good and/or bad qualities one has, one will, with the frictions arising from the very energy of those qualities, reduce oneself to dust at the standard rate. Gleckner:

> Man's violence ultimately produces his own defeat or decay, but what is more important is that man's virtues – courage, pride, love, loyalty – also lead him to destruction ... And it is this "immutable law" which Byron seeks to dramatize for the first time in *The Giaour* ...

In finding expression for that "immutable law", Byron placed himself in a region of magnificent remoteness from the political concerns of other writers. The reader may attempt to trace Byron's predecessors, finding here and there recollections of Shakespeare, Milton, Pope or Congreve, but in the main the effect produced by those masters on Byron's own is insufficient to explain Byron's greatness. The real truth is that Byron was the follower of no man. He accomplished what was born within him, what had to be put into practice because it was the expression of that energy which brought him a long way. It felt to him as if everything in life was necessary and ineluctable. As Ernest Hartley Coleridge would say in his introductory memoir to *The Poetical Works of Lord Byron* (1905):

> There is "something" as [Byron] might have said, in *The Giaour* ... which was not derived from books, or noted by the tourist in search of the picturesque. He had plunged into deep waters and seen strange sights below the surface of the wave.

Byron's pessimism (as Gleckner reminds us, "neither cynical nor predestinarian") is made more poignant by the restless apperceptions of a nervous system altogether modern in its morbid sensitiveness. His work is painful, haunted by human love and human vices, and by abominations committed without enthusiasm, without hope:

The Mind, that broods o'er guilty woes,
Is like the Scorpion girt by fire;
In circle narrowing as it glows
The flames around their captive close,
Till inly searched by thousand throes,
And maddening in her ire,
One sad and sole relief she knows –
The sting she nourished for her foes,
Whose venom never was in vain,
Gives but one pang, and cures all pain,
And darts into her desperate brain. –
So do the dark in soul expire,
Or live like Scorpion girt by fire;
So writhes the mind Remorse hath riven,
Unfit for earth, undoomed for heaven,
Darkness above, despair beneath,
Around it flame, within it death!

(422-438)

Yet "Byron's romanticism ... was only half sincere ... [and] The world insisted on simplifying him, and omitting the element of pose in his cosmic despair ..." (*History of Western Philosophy*, 721.)

The looseness of style allows a voracious openness to the flow of inexact rhymes ("beneath" and "death") and repeated phrases ("Scorpion girt by fire"), and it all blends into something like an incantation. There breathes from the above passage, so despairing and so erudite (Byron's allusion to the ancient legend of the self-destructive scorpion), a strange magic, a sorcery that can move any reader who has ever been troubled by deep regret and guilt for some misdeed to the bottom of his soul. The Giaour slays Hassan, decapitating him, but somehow not extinguishing him entirely:

His [Hassan's] breast with wounds unnumbered riven,
His back to earth, his face to Heaven,
Fall'n Hassan lies – his unclosed eye
Yet lowering on his enemy,
As if the hour that sealed his fate
Surviving left his quenchless hate;
And o'er him bends that foe with brow
As dark as his that bled below.

(667-674)

In the last two lines of the above passage, Byron deliberately blurs the distinction between conquering hero and vanquished foe, because he knows that both will soon rot and resolve indistinguishably into the ecosystem.

As the Giaour makes his confession to the Friar, before dying of his wounds, there is an image of remorse which will have a reverberating impact upon such later writers as Baudelaire and Edgar Allen Poe (1809-1849):

> It is as if the dead could feel
> The icy worm around them steal,
> And shudder, as the reptiles creep
> To revel o'er their rotting sleep,
> Without the power to scare away
> The cold consumers of their clay!
>
> *(The Giaour*, 945-950)

Byron's pessimistic vision is rich, gorgeous, cerebral and disturbed. Whereas in Johnson's world one could:

> Fall in the gen'ral massacre of gold;
> Wide-wasting pest! that rages unconfined,
> And crowds with crimes the records of mankind ...
>
> ('The Vanity of Human Wishes'),

in Byron's universe all energy seems to gravitate one towards the personalised charnel-house:

> Dark as to thee my deeds may seem –
> My memory now is but the tomb
> Of joys long dead ...
>
> *(The Giaour*, 999-1001)

In Byron's view, one could find oneself in a powerless position, forced to "bear a life of lingering woes" (1003), and "to sustain/The searching throes of ceaseless pain." (1005) precisely because, as there is no structure of things, one's mind will spin its own structure, with or without its owner's leave. Poetry will not come when called, and guilt will not go when shooed. The plates of the Italian engraver, Giovanni Battista Piranesi (1720-1778), showed surreal representations of vast classical dungeons, with endlessly labyrinthine combinations of staircases. In *Confessions of an English Opium-Eater*, De Quincey would famously compare the visions of Piranesi with the self-replicating twistings and turnings of his own troubled conscience:

> With the same power of endless growth and self-reproduction
> did my architecture proceed in dreams ...

But De Quincey was a Christian (albeit an eccentric one), with the moral duty to inform his readers that, although taking opium can be fun initially, the repercussions are so awful that it is not worth the candle. In contrast to that, when Byron's lucubration brings him, and his readers, within the pull of any black hole, it is not his Christian duty to prejudice and redirect that lucubration. Half horrified, half exhilarated, the reader is carried along (and sometimes dropped) by the poet, enchanted and repelled by the narrative blend: half fun, half cruelty. One thinks of J.M. Barrie's (1860-1937) Peter Pan taking the Darling children on a night flight but not appearing at all worried about their welfare:

> ... they were sleepy; and that was a danger, for the moment they popped off, down they fell. The awful thing was that Peter thought this funny.
>
> "There he goes again!" he would cry gleefully, as Michael suddenly dropped like a stone.
>
> "Save him, save him!" cried Wendy, looking with horror at the cruel sea far below. Eventually Peter would dive through the air, and catch Michael just before he could strike the sea, and it was lovely the way he did it; but he always waited till the last moment, and you felt it was his cleverness that interested him and not the saving of human life. Also he was fond of variety, and the sport that engrossed him one moment would suddenly cease to engage him, so there was always the possibility that the next time you fell he would let you go.
>
> (*Peter Pan* [1911], Chapter Four)

Byron's tales are mediated to us via narrators whose identities are not fixed. The Byronic style concurs with the content: everything – the self, poetry, politics, the world, the universe – is disputable.

Byron's poetry is often like a facetious illustration of the philosopher David Hume's (1711-1776) theory, that the self is no more than "a bundle or collection of different perspectives, which ... are in perpetual flux and movement" (*A Treatise of Human Nature* [1740], Book II, Part IV, Section vi). Byron irresponsibly implicates the reader in a troublesome sociability of alternative perspectives.

In Byron's view, there is no pattern to which we must adapt ourselves. We are, insofar as we know, alone, and therefore we must *make do*. When people perceive the universe to be godless, they tend to feel themselves subjected to unendurable agonies. Better to give a god full authority to sweep away all scorpion-venom and other pollutants. That is why people seek to admit the flow of Christian, Kantian, Wordsworthian, or some other way of thinking into their lives. Therefore, the content and style of Byron's work is infused with the ache to be without such prescribed precincts. In *Beppo* (1818), Byron would flaunt the idea that he is making it up as he goes along:

> I've half a mind to tumble down to prose,
> But verse is more in fashion – so here goes!
>
> (52)

There is only self-creativity and then death. It is better to imagine the universe not as a set of facts, nor a collection of lumps in space, nor three-dimensional entities bound together by certain unbreakable relations as taught by physics, chemistry or other natural sciences. The universe is a process which Byron thinks of as hostile to man. If man tries to trick it, or organise it, or feel at home in it, or make some kind of cosy pattern in which he can rest, the process will inevitably overthrow his efforts. In such a place, human notions, such as the notion of honour, or esteem, seem pathetic:

> I've braved [danger] – not for Honour's boast;
> I smile at laurels won or lost. –
> To such let others carve their way,
> For high renown, or hireling pay ...
>
> (1012-1015)

All generalisations about the universe, all patterns put upon it, are forms of distortion. To ignore that, to evade it, to attempt to see the processes of the universe as submissive to some kind of intellectualism, to some sort of plan, to attempt to draw up a set of rules or a set of laws, or a formula, is a form of self-indulgence and stupidity. Whenever you try to understand anything by whatever powers you have, you will discover that you are trying to apply a formula to something that evades your formula because whenever you try to nail it down, new abysses open, and then those abysses open and there are other abysses. Politics offers the most rigorous generalisations of, to Byron, the most external and empty kind. Jerome McGann has noted the following about Byron:

> Politics, even individual human actions, are seen [by Byron] as manifestations of a larger, and fundamentally natural, life force. Vendetta and assassination were common occurrences in Italy, Byron observed, and he frequently mentions these things in his letters and journals as if they were forms of natural calamity rather than moral goods or evils.
>
> (*Fiery Dust*, 214 note)

Love, not politics, was the force that motivated the Giaour to kill Hassan. The Giaour/Byron represents a depth, an elsewhere, unanswerable by schooled thinking. 'God' and 'Alla' provide blanket explanations for the west and east respectively:

> "Yes, Love indeed is light from Heaven, –
> A spark of that immortal fire
> With angels shared, by Alla given,
> To lift from earth our low desire ...
>
> (1131-1134)

Byron later chronicles the intellectual development of Don Juan, who, if he were alive today, would ponder the sort of questions tackled by Stephen Law in *The Philosophy Gym* (2003). Is time travel possible? Could a machine think? Does God exist? Where did the universe come from? But however strenuous one's intellectual labours, one's hunger for something *other* rarely diminishes underneath. In the following passage, Byron surveys the superficial aestheticism behind youth's furrowed brow, and then finds with a dash ("–") the precise spot at which to chisel it all off with one tap:

He thought about himself, and the whole earth,
Of man the wonderful, and of the stars,
And how the deuce they ever could have birth;
And then he thought of earthquakes, and of wars,
How many miles the moon might have in girth,
Of air-balloons, and of the many bars
To perfect knowledge of the boundless skies –
And then he thought of Donna Julia's eyes.

(*Don Juan*, I, 92)

Now *there* (the last line of the above) is an avenue of enquiry for a young man! Don Juan has not been brought down to earth with a merely carnal bump. The dash has not – as people who do not understand Byron unthinkingly assume – merely introduced a vulgar surprise to debunk Don Juan's nascent philosophising. It has redirected the reader's attention to the thing that really matters, to the thing that means the most, but can be explained the least. That thing is love. Byron has, a little earlier in *Don Juan*, already told the reader about Donna Julia's eyes:

Her eye (I'm very fond of handsome eyes)
Was large and dark, suppressing half its fire
Until she spoke, then through its soft disguise
Flashed an expression more of pride than ire,
And love than either; and there would arise
A something in them which was not desire,
But would have been, perhaps, but for the soul
Which struggled through and chastened down the whole.

(I, 60)

Her glossy hair was clustered o'er a brow
Bright with intelligence, and fair, and smooth;
Her eyebrow's shape was like the aërial bow,
Her cheek all purple with the beam of youth,
Mounting, at times, to a transparent glow,
As if her veins ran lightning; she, in sooth,
Possessed an air and grace by no means common ...

(I, 61)

The protean narrative gives the reader the sense of the magic space in which love's unaccountable tendrils will joyously entwine the couple.

Byron's heart was sick within him, but his courage as a writer did not fail him. He was, as Russell says, "fierce" (*History of Western Philosophy*, 721). He took cognisance of the reality of the world, and that the foul flood was spreading and drowning in its pestilential morass the world of weak, corruptible people. But he knew love, and he knew its power was uplifting. He knew, too, like James Reeves in the mid-20th century, that his poetry would cause embarrassment amongst its readers: "It seems ... embarrassing to be alive. It seems naïve to indulge in private feelings. But without them existence is pointless." (Introduction to Reeves' *Collected Poems: 1929-1959*.) Byron's vision was by no means composed entirely of excrescences pulling him hellwards. It would take a Poe to refine that specific morbidity in Byron, and to aggravate that specific bizarreness:

> It may be asserted, without hesitation, that *no* event is so terribly well adapted to inspire the supremeness of bodily and of mental distress, as is burial before death. The unendurable oppression of the lungs – the stifling fumes of the damp earth – the clinging to the death garments – the rigid embrace of the narrow house – the blackness of the absolute Night – the silence like a sea that overwhelms – the unseen but palpable presence of the Conqueror Worm – these things, with thoughts of the air and grass above, with memory of dear friends who would fly to save us if but informed of our fate, and with consciousness that of this fate they can *never* be informed – that our hopeless portion is that of the really dead – these considerations, I say, carry into the heart, which still palpitates, a degree of appalling and intolerable horror from which the most daring imagination must recoil. We know of nothing so agonising upon Earth – we can dream of nothing half so hideous in the realms of the nethermost Hell. And thus all narratives upon this topic have an interest profound ...
>
> ('The Premature Burial')

Whereas Poe persisted in cultivating his imaginative creations' extremeness, and in plunging the reader into abysses containing unexamined horrors (such as "detestable putrescence"), Byron's humanity was often implicit in his sympathy with the emotional wounds that individuals inwardly sustain:

Alas! the breast that inly bleeds
Hath nought to dread from outward blow –
Who falls from all he knows of bliss,
Cares little into what abyss.

(1155-1158)

Byron followed the promptings not just of his melancholy, but also of his sense of humour, and so it was that when, in exile, he found his balance between those two apparent opposites, many people saw him as most perilously unbalanced.

The Vision of Judgment

As Poet Laureate, Southey produced a long and ridiculous poem, *A Vision of Judgment* (1821), about King George III's entry into heaven:

O'er the adamantine gates an Angel stood on the summit.
Ho! he exclaimed, King George of England cometh to
    judgement!
Hear Heaven! Ye Angels hear! Souls of the good and the
Wicked
Whom it concerns, attend!

There was, really, no need for Byron to attack the poem. So many contemporaries were pointing at it in hilarious disbelief. To give one example, Hartley Coleridge (1796-1849), who was often diffident to the point of characterlessness, expressed his opinion about Southey's poem with considerable force, in a letter to his brother, Derwent Coleridge, in 1821:

Have you seen Southey's Vision of Judgement!!!!! *O Tempora, O Mores* – And is it come to this? And our good dear mother gave me such a hint to praise in her last letter!!! I came off, I think, pretty well, saying that I did not think it the *best* of S.'s poems. Seriously speaking, our late lamented Monarch did not deserve such an insult to his memory. And who, but a converted Revolutionist, would ever have dream'd of spurring the wind-gall'd, glander'd, stagger'd, bott-begrown, spavin'd... broken-down gelding, that has turn'd blind with facing year after year the same round of Court Compliments – who, I say, but the Hexameter long trot; and so mounted as on another Rosinante, set off in search of adventures, in the world of spirits?

"Hexameter long trot" alludes to Southey's bizarre determination to use the classical hexameter, unsuited to the English language and therefore scarcely used in England. Southey, taking his Laureateship very seriously, was one of Hazlitt's favourite targets. Paulin encapsulates Hazlitt's view of Southey well:

> ... Southey is neither subtle nor wildly imaginative; he's an unreconstructed Jacobin who is just as fanatical in the service of his new political creed. His extreme monarchist sentiments everywhere betray his deeply rooted Jacobin principles, a fixed and callow ideology which makes him appear in Hazlitt's prose as a rigid, mechanically active figure. A writer who passes from verse to prose, history to poetry, he seems to work by the clock, and is as stiffly definite as the umbrella he always carries on his visits to London.
> (*The Day-Star of Liberty: William Hazlitt's Radical Style*, 171-12)

Byron was not aroused until he had read the paragraphs in Southey's preface that attacked "lascivious" poets:

> ... Men of diseased hearts and depraved imaginations, who, forming a system of opinions to suit their own unhappy course of conduct, have rebelled against the holiest ordinances of human society, and hating that revealed religion which, with all their efforts and bravadoes, they are unable entirely to disbelieve, labour to make others as miserable as themselves, by infecting men with a moral virus that eats into the soul! The school which they have set up may properly be called the Satanic school ...

In September 1821, Byron stepped in, invoking the words of Pope like a counter-spell to the evils emanating from sycophancy:

> It has been wisely said, that "One fool makes many;" and it hath been poetically observed –
>
> "[That] fools rush in where angels fear to tread."
> [POPE'S *Essay on Criticism*, line 625]

If Mr. Southey had not rushed in where he had no business, and where he never was before, and never will be again, the following poem would not have been written. It is not impossible that it may be as good as his own, seeing that it cannot, by any species of stupidity, natural or acquired, be *worse*. The gross flattery, the dull impudence, the renegado intolerance, and impious cant, of the poem by the author of "Wat Tyler", are something so stupendous as to form the sublime of himself – containing the quintessence of his own attributes.

Having set the spectacle of Southey stewing in his own wrongness – "I say nothing of the cowardice of such [sycophancy]; its meanness speaks for itself" – Byron sets himself up (in a postscript) as part of literary tradition, and therefore exempt from the sort of crass censure in which the Southeys of the world indulge:

> P.S. – It is possible that some readers may object, in these objectionable times, to the freedom with which saints, angels, and spiritual persons discourse in this *Vision*. But, for precedents upon such points, I must refer him to Fielding's *Journey from this World to the next*, and to the Visions of myself, the said Quevedo, in Spanish or translated. The reader is also requested to observe, that no doctrinal tenets are insisted upon or discussed; that the person of the Deity is carefully withheld from sight, which is more than can be said for the Laureate, who hath thought proper to make him talk, not "like a school-divine," but like the un-scholarlike Mr.Southey. The whole action passes on the outside of heaven; and Chaucer's *Wife of Bath*, Pulci's *Morgante Maggiore*, Swift's *Tale of a Tub*, and the other works above referred to, are cases in point of the freedom with which saints, etc., may be permitted to converse in works not intended to be serious.

In *Don Juan*, VII, Byron would say something similar:

> They accuse me – *Me* – the present writer of
> The present poem – of – I know not what –
> A tendency to under-rate and scoff
> At human power and virtue, and all that;
> And this they say in language rather rough.

Good God! I wonder what they would be at!
I say no more than hath been said in Danté's
Verse, and by Solomon and by Cervantes;

(VII, 3)

By Swift, by Machiavel, by Rochefoucalt,
By Fénélon, by Luther, and by Plato;
By Tillotson, and Wesley, and Rousseau,
Who knew this life was not worth a potato.
'Tis not their fault, not mine, if this be so …

(VII, 4)

Straight after the preface to his *Vision*, Byron avails himself of
the opportunity he has just awarded himself to be lightly blasph-
emous. He outlines heaven as a civil service environment, with Saint
Peter as a sort of under-worked chief security guard/petty bureaucrat,
"yawn[ing]" (17) by the "celestial gate" (16). St Peter's obtuse and
uneducated enquiries as to the identity of the latest arrival illustrate
the momentum with which Byron's humour far outstrips Southey's
rectitude:

But ere he could return to his repose,
A Cherub flapped his right wing o'er his eyes –
At which Saint Peter yawned, and rubbed his nose:
"Saint porter," said the angel, "prithee rise!"
Waving a goodly wing, which glowed, as glows
An earthly peacock's tail, with heavenly dyes:
To which the saint replied, "Well, what's the matter?
Is Lucifer come back with all this clatter?"

(17)

"No," quoth the Cherub; "George the Third is dead."
"And who *is* George the Third?" replied the apostle:
"*What George? What Third?*" "The King of England," said
The angel. "Well! he wont find kings to jostle
Him on his way; but does he wear his head?
Because the last we saw here had a tustle,
And ne'er would have got into Heaven's good graces,
Had he not flung his head in all our faces.

(18)

Byron has the members of the heavenly host looking a little bored at their workstations, toying idly with heavenly components (as office workers at a loose end might twiddle with items of stationery):

> The Angels all were singing out of tune,
> And hoarse with having little else to do,
> Excepting to wind up the sun and moon,
> Or curb a runaway young star or two ...
>
> (2)

Byron knowingly situates his Satan in a pseudo-Miltonic cosmos:

> Then Satan turned and waved his swarthy hand,
> Which stirred with its electric qualities
> Clouds farther off than we can understand,
> Although we find him sometimes in our skies;
> Infernal thunder shook both sea and land
> In all the planets – and Hell's batteries
> Let off the artillery, which Milton mentions
> As one of Satan's most sublime inventions.
>
> (52)

Byron maintains his narrative omniscience with hammy winks to the reader, but his intention is serious, and he means the poem to be like a fairground mirror in which society's distortions can be made straight. Hence, his commentary on the funeral of George III:

> ... Of all
> The fools who flocked to swell or see the show,
> Who cared about the corpse? The funeral
> Made the attraction, and the black the woe.
> There throbbed not there a thought which pierced the pall;
> And when the gorgeous coffin was laid low,
> It seemed the mockery of hell to fold
> The rottenness of eighty years in gold.
>
> (10)

With typically mischievous ambivalence, Byron refers not just to the dissolution and putrefaction of the corpse left behind by George III ('rottenness'), but also to the political corruption that has taken hold of England under that king's reign. The reign was long: "He came to his sceptre young; he leaves it old" (XLIII). The legacy of oppressiveness will "stink", as it were, until the deliquescence has been allowed to run its course, and until all pockets of vice and woe are dissolved. With such thoroughness the entire aberration will be reduced to inoffensive nothingness, but, regrettably, in Byron's view, the process will take time:

> So mix his body with the dust! It might
> Return to what it *must* far sooner, were
> The natural compound left alone to fight
> Its way back into earth, and fire, and air ...
>
> (11)

Byron suggests that the efforts to preserve the royal body are synonymous with efforts to preserve bad kingship:

> But the unnatural balsams merely blight
> What Nature made him at his birth, as bare
> As the mere million's base unmummied clay –
> Yet all his spices but prolong decay.
>
> (11)

When Byron attacks Southey, he attacks hypocrisy, because Southey is the very essence of that vice:

> He first sank to the bottom – like his works,
> But soon rose to the surface – like himself;
> For all corrupted things are buoyed like corks,
> By their own rottenness ...
>
> (105)

At the height of the controversy over Byron's *Vision*, he wrote to Kinnaird on 2 May 1822:

> As to myself, I shall not be deterred by an outcry. They hate me, and I detest them, I mean your present public, but they shall not interrupt the march of my mind, nor prevent me from telling the tyrants who are attempting to trample upon all thought, that their thrones will yet be rocked to their foundation.
>
> (*Correspondence*, II, 223.)

That letter is important with regard to our understanding of Byron's motivation for writing *The Vision*. He is not seeking merely to even the score with an adversary. He is fighting evil. Southey is evil because he eulogises a monarch and a regime responsible for deaths in America, France and Ireland. The concept of freedom has been diabolically – and, for Byron, unacceptably – reconfigured in Southey's *Vision* to look like something abhorrent in the mob:

> And in the hubbub of senseless sounds the watchwords of
>   faction,
> Freedom, Invaded Rights, Corruption, and War, and
> Oppression
> Loudly enounced were heard ...

Remarkably, Southey had once been a fanatical supporter of Robespierre, and declared, on hearing the news of Robespierre's death, that he would rather have heard of his own father's death and thought it "the worst misfortune mankind could have sustained." Knowledge of the fact that Southey's father was already dead helps to reveal something important, if commonplace: the personal malleability that makes the shift from one extreme to another possible. The Byron of *The Vision of Judgement* would give Southey much more reason to be fearful than the Byron of *English Bards and Scotch Reviewers* did.

Southey's *Vision*, evokes the spectacle of the prompt, loyal Laureate attempting to squeeze through the pearly gates with the royal family:

> But the weight of the body withheld me. I stoopt to the
>   fountain,
> Eager to drink thereof, and to put away all that was earthly.
> Darkness came over me then at the chilling touch of the
>   water,
> And my feet methought sunk, and I fell precipitate. Starting
> Then I awoke ...

Byron's *Vision* evokes the more recognisable spectacle of Southey the hanger-on, the scavenger, animated purely by vanity, ingratiating and utterly without scruples:

The varlet was not an ill-favoured knave;
A good deal like a vulture in the face,
With a hook nose and a hawk's eye, which gave
 A smart and sharper-looking sort of grace
To his whole aspect, which, though rather grave,
Was by no means so ugly as his case;
But that, indeed, was hopeless as can be,
Quite a poetic felony "*de se*."

(94)

Byron has Southey "plead[ing] his own bad cause,/With all the attitudes of self-applause." (95) Byron witheringly summarises what Southey's plaints would be likely to sound like if he were compelled to appeal to the heavenly tribunal:

He said – (I only give the heads) – he said,
He meant no harm in scribbling; 'twas his way
Upon all topics; 'twas, besides, his bread,
Of which he buttered both sides; 'twould delay
Too long the assembly (he was pleased to dread),
And take up rather more time than a day,
To name his works – he would but cite a few –
"Wat Tyler" – "Rhymes on Blenheim" – "Waterloo."

(96)

Southey's *Vision* affected an elaborate salute over the coffin of George III. Byron's counter-blast left the thick fumes of sarcasm. Is there no beginning to our Laureate's integrity?

He had written praises of a regicide;
He had written praises of all kings whatever;
He had written for republics far and wide,
And then against them bitterer than ever;
For pantisocracy he once had cried
Aloud, a scheme less moral than 'twas clever;
Then grew a hearty anti-jacobin –
Had turned his coat – and would have turned his skin.

(97)

Is there no beginning to his talents?

> He had sung against all battles, and again
> In their high praise and glory; he had called
> Reviewing "the ungentle craft," and then
> Became as base a critic as e'er crawled –
> Fed, paid, and pampered by the very men
> By whom his muse and morals had been mauled:
> He had written much blank verse, and blanker prose,
> And more of both than any body knows.
>
> (98)

With a masterstroke, Byron has Southey, the biographer, place himself at Satan's disposal:

> He had written Wesley's life: – here turning round
> To Satan, "Sir, I'm ready to write yours,
> In two octavo volumes, nicely bound,
> With notes and preface, all that most allures
> The pious purchaser; and there's no ground
> For fear, for I can choose my own reviewers:
> So let me have the proper documents,
> That I may add you to my other saints."
>
> (99)

Byron's indignation at Southey's double-dealing is exquisitely controlled. The poem contains intense anger, and yet has, at the same time, such a light touch that the blend is unique.

Manfred (A Drama)

> E.J. Trelawney records that in 1822 Byron told Shelley of the criticisms John Murray, Byron's publisher, had of his dramas. Murray thought them unstageable and, worse, unmarketable, and urged Byron in the double interest of art and commerce to resume his "Corsair style, to please the ladies."
>
> (Frank D. McConnell, 'Byron as Antipoet')

Byron's *Manfred* (1817), the verse play that inspired Schumann's musical poem and Tchaikovsky's *Manfred* symphony, was written in the wake of war across Europe. The dawn following the night of the Napoleonic wars did not bring peace and stability. Instead, it ushered in an age of revolutions, and an explosion of nationalist fervour, fuelled by economic recession and widespread shortages of food. Empires crumbled, as charismatic leaders liberated old nations and forged new ones. It seemed as if the outer storms compelled artists to turn inward, and there find a counterforce against the forces breaking in so frightfully from without. This collision of romanticism in the arts with nationalism on the streets produced two kinds of hero: the contemplative, self-regarding individualist and the active revolutionary socialist – one hero fighting with outer conflicts; the other wrestling with inner conflicts. Byron's Manfred typifies that introspective, romantic hero, the reclusive who shut himself away from society because of a dreadful, but unnamed deed that caused the death of his beloved:

> My solitude is solitude no more,
> But peopled with the Furies – I have gnashed
> My teeth in darkness till returning morn,
> Then cursed myself till sunset – I have prayed
> For madness as a blessing – 'tis denied me.
> I have affronted Death – but in the war
> Of elements the waters shrunk from me,
> And fatal things passed harmless – the cold hand
> Of an all-pitiless Demon held me back,
> Back by a single hair, which would not break
> In Fantasy, Imagination, all
> The affluence of my soul – which one day was
> A Crœsus in creation – I plunged deep,
> But, like an ebbing wave, it dashed me back
> Into the gulf of unfathomed thought ...
>
> (II, 130-144)

Manfred looks only for death, but death on his own terms, not mediated by the dogma of the Christian church, nor ordained by the powerful spirits of nature, nor damned by demons. One thinks of Napoleon:

> My mistress is power. I have given too much to its conquest
> to let it be taken from me, or even suffer anyone to covet it.
>
> (to Roederer, 4th November 1804)

Manfred pits his individual human will against all three powers and wins. He wins because in the tradition of the romantic artist hero, he has reached his own enlightenment by treading a path of personal suffering, as the Spirits of Destiny acknowledge:

> ... This man
> Is of no common order, as his port
> And presence here denote; his sufferings
> Have been of an immortal nature, like
> Our own; his knowledge and his powers and will,
> As far as is compatible with clay,
> Which clogs the ethereal essence, have been such
> As clay hath seldom borne; his aspirations
> Have been beyond the dwellers of the earth,
> And they have only taught him what we know –
> That knowledge is not happiness, and science
> But an exchange of ignorance for that
> Which is another kind of ignorance.
>
> (Act II, scene 3, 51-63)

Critics have seen much of Byron's own life in the character of Manfred: his wilfulness, his passion, his despair, even his incestuous love affair with his half-sister, Augusta, which some suggest may be the unnamed deed that drives Manfred to suicide. Mario Praz has argued provocatively that the affinities between Byron and the Marquis de Sade (1740-1814) are very strong:

> What Manfred said of Astarte ('I loved her, and destroy'd her'), what Byron wished to be able to say of Augusta and of Annabella (see the Incantation in *Manfred*), was to become the motto of the 'fatal' heroes of Romantic literature. They diffuse all round them the curse which weighs upon their destiny, they blast, like the simoom, those who have the misfortune to meet with them (the image is from *Manfred*, III. I); they destroy themselves, and destroy the unlucky women who come within their orbit. Their relations with their mistresses are those of an incubus-devil with his victim.
>
> (*The Romantic Agony* [1933])

In a weary letter from Italy, Byron tells Augusta that despite his love of nature, even the spectacular scenery fails to console him:

The mountains, the glacier, the forest nor the cloud can for
one moment lighten the weight upon my heart, nor enable me
to lose my own wretched identity in the majesty and power
and the glory around, above, beneath me.

Russell has written interestingly about Byron's relationship with
Augusta:

> His shyness and sense of friendlessness made him look for
> comfort in love affairs, but as he was unconsciously seeking
> a mother rather than a mistress, all disappointed him except
> Augusta. Calvinism, which he never shook off ... made him
> feel that his manner of life was wicked; but wickedness, he
> told himself, was a hereditary curse in his blood, an evil fate
> to which he was predestined by the Almighty. If that were
> indeed the case, since he *must* be remarkable, he would be
> remarkable as a sinner, and would dare transgressions beyond
> the courage of the fashionable libertines whom he wished to
> despise. He loved Augusta genuinely because she was of his
> blood ... and also, more simply, because she had an elder
> sister's kindly care for his daily welfare. But this was not all
> she had to offer him. Through her simplicity and her obliging
> good-nature, she became the means of providing him with
> the most delicious self-congratulatory remorse. He could feel
> himself the equal of the greatest sinners – the peer of Manfred
> ...

(*History of Western Philosophy*, 718)

Though he was the embodiment of the melancholic romantic hero,
Byron was that other hero too, the man of action. In 1820 he joined
the Italian freedom fighters, the Carbonari movement (against
Austrian rule), and a few years later became involved with the Greek
struggle for independence. *Manfred* echoes the revolutionary times
in a speech by Nemesis, ruler of the Spirits of Destiny, who has an
excuse for her late arrival:

> I was detained repairing shattered thrones,
> Marrying fools, restoring dynasties,
> Avenging men upon their enemies,
> And making them repent their own revenge;
> Goading the wise to madness; from the dull

Shaping out oracles to rule the world
Afresh – for they were waxing out of date,
And mortals dared to ponder for themselves,
To weigh kings in the balance, and to speak
Of Freedom, the forbidden fruit.

(*Manfred*, Act II, scene 3, 62-71)

As that forbidden fruit of freedom was grasped, albeit precariously, by the heroic leaders of Europe, many countries looked to their own histories with a refurbished sense of pride, and began to resurrect half-neglected national heroes. Though he was finally defeated at the Battle of Waterloo, Napoleon's achievements as an administrator turned out to be of lasting significance and include the *Code Napoléon*, which remains the basis of French law.

Beppo

With all its sinful doings, I must say,
That Italy's a pleasant place to me,
Who love to see the Sun shine every day ...

(41)

I like on Autumn evenings to ride out,
Without being forc'd to bid my groom be sure
My cloak is round his middle strapp'd about,
Because the skies are not the most secure;
I know too that, if stopp'd upon my route,
Where the green alleys windingly allure,
Reeling with *grapes* red waggons choke the way, –
In England 'twould be dung, dust, or a dray.

(42)

Beppo (1818) shows that Byron prefers Italy to England. It also shows that Byron will not follow the example of other romantic poets who had got hold of philosophical tenets and tried to combine the authentic lyrical spasm with a metaphysical explanation of the universe.

Beppo was the poem in which Byron made comic, rather than hid, his difficulty in finding rhymes for the *ottava rima* metre. He began to twist the necks of accepted epithets in order to make poetry splutter and screech instead of twittering:

I love the language, that soft bastard Latin,
Which melts like kisses from a female mouth,
And sounds as if it should be writ on satin,
With syllables which breathe of the sweet South,
And gentle liquids gliding all so pat in,
That not a single accent seems uncouth,
Like our harsh northern whistling, grunting, gutteral,
Which we're oblig'd to hiss, and spit, and sputter all.

(44)

Having been through a dark period ("The momentous crisis of his personal life had coincided with that of Europe itself" [*Byron: A Literary Life*, 91]), he found a new lightness with which he could respond to his environment:

Didst ever see a Gondola? For fear
You should not, I'll describe it you exactly:
'Tis a long covered boat that's common here,
Carved at the prow, built lightly, but compactly,
Rowed by two rowers, each called 'Gondolier',
It glides along the water looking blackly,
Just like a coffin clapt in a canoe,
Where none can make out what you say or do.

(19)

The poem is modelled on the style of the serio-comic Italian poet, Luigi Pulci (1432-84), whose masterpiece is the *Morgante Maggiore* (1483). Byron had actually caught the spirit of Pulci via a poem by John Hookam Frere (alias 'Whistlecraft'), *The Monks and the Giants*. Byron saw the potential in "Whistlecraft's"/Pulci's inclusion of the gamut of responses to the world, from the serious to the ludicrous. Byron had found the perfect vehicle in which he could practice a newly nimble disrespect for anything with hypocrisy in it:

She was a married woman; 'tis convenient,
Because in Christian countries 'tis a rule
To view their little slips with eyes more lenient;
Whereas if single ladies play the fool,
(Unless within the period intervenient
A well-timed wedding makes the scandal cool)

I don't know how they ever can get over it.
Except they manage never to discover it.

(24)

Byron wrote *Beppo* during September and early October 1817. He wrote to Murray on 12th October:

> I have written a poem (of 84 octave stanzas) humorous, in or after the excellent manner of Mr Whistlecraft (whom I take to be Frere), on a Venetian anecdote which amused me.

The amusing anecdote was that a man had been away at sea for so long that his wife believed him to be dead. However, the man returned to find his wife and her new lover at a ball. To conclude the anecdote, all three had coffee at the new lover's house. That simple plot suited Byron's imagination in the same way that a large, uncluttered stage might suit a brilliant, restless, undisciplined solo dancer. Byron's heterogeneous, hyperactive thoughts are allowed to find intelligible and easy expression, and even unfold and move about with grace in *Beppo*. The mode of expression has unbuttoned itself (rather is as if the poet were in Levantine or Oriental dress, or were employing some other sartorial expression of disdain for convention, such as the eschewing of elaborate cravats, leaving his shirt-neck open, or even leaving off his coat altogether and wearing shirt-sleeves). *Beppo* displays Byron creating and inhabiting the verbal element in which he can best perform. No writer before Byron had ever referred to *Macbeth* humorously, but Byron points out that if the reader is thinking of coming to Venice as a recognisable non-Catholic, he will risk being "haul[ed] ... o'er the coals" by the clergy, who will "No[t] say one mass to cool the cauldron's bubble/That boiled your bones unless you paid them double." There is such a sense of relish in the poet's candour. He runs amok, saying just what he likes about, say, the transparently brutal Catholic fanaticism in Italy, or the ridiculous charade acted out, back in England, by young Protestant women:

> 'Tis true, your budding Miss is very charming,
> But shy and awkward at first coming out,
> So much alarmed, that she is quite alarming,
> All Giggle, Blush – half Pertness, and half Pout;
> And glancing at *Mamma*, for fear there's harm in

What you, she, it, or they, may be about:
The Nursery still lisps out in all they utter –
Besides, they always smell of bread and butter.

(39)

The poetic fountain has begun to overflow, and Byron will not try to regulate it, but will allow himself be buffeted from the gay to the grave:

I fear I have a little turn for Satire,
And yet methinks the older that one grows
Inclines us more to laugh than scold, though Laughter
Leaves us so doubly serious shortly after.

(79)

He would indicate his fondness for England by alluding to William Cowper's (1731-1800) poem, *The Task*, II, and Charles Churchill's (1731-1764) poem, 'The Farewell' ("Be England what she will,/With all her faults, she is my Country still."), and then allow it to become comically apparent that, as he likes everything, it must follow that his fondness for his country means nothing at all:

'England! with all thy faults I love thee still,'
I said at Calais, and have not forgot it;
I like to speak and lucubrate my fill;
I like the government (but that is not it);
I like the freedom of the press and quill;
I like the Habeas Corpus (when we've got it);
I like a Parliamentary debate,
Particularly when it's not too late;

(47)

I like the taxes, when they're not too many;
I like a seacoal fire, when not too dear;
I like a beef-steak, too, as well as any;
Have no objection to a pot of beer;
I like the weather, when it is not rainy,
That is, I like two months of every year.
And so God save the Regent, Church, and King!
Which means that I like all and every thing.

(48)

He then begins to enumerate his "beloved" country's "little" blemishes, and does so for the length of another stanza before "repudiating" himself for his digression:

> Our [England's] standing army, and disbanded seamen,
> Poor's rate, Reform, my own, the nation's debt,
> Our little riots, just to show we are free men,
> Our trifling bankruptcies in the Gazette,
> Our cloudy climate, and our chilly women,
> All these I can forgive, and those forget,
> And greatly venerate our recent glories,
> And wish they were not owing to the Tories.
>
> (49)

> But to my tale of Laura, – for I find
> Digression is a sin ...
>
> (50)

Digression, like sin, is at the heart of Byron's work, like a gemlike paradox: not only can digression serve as structure; it in fact constitutes the very structure of human consciousness:

> 96
> Of the Immortality of the Soul, it appears to me that there can be little doubt, if we attend for a moment to the action of the Mind. It is in perpetual activity. I used to doubt of it, but reflection has taught me better. It acts also very independent of body; in dreams for instance incoherently and madly, I grant you; but still it is *Mind*, and much more *Mind* than when we are awake ...
>
> (*Detached Thoughts*)

His knowledge of that reality gives Byron the confidence that his poetry does possess the wealth and weight of thought that gives brevity to his style, making it concise and pregnant. He discusses digression in another digression:

> ... by degrees [digression]
> Becomes exceeding tedious to my mind,
> And, therefore, may the reader too displease –
> The gentle reader, who may wax unkind,

And caring little for the Author's ease,
Insist on knowing what he means, a hard
And hapless situation for a Bard.

(50)

In yet another digression, he hammily laments the limitations on his
talents as a poet:

Oh that I had the art of easy writing
What should be easy reading! could I scale
Parnassus, where the Muses sit inditing
Those pretty poems never known to fail,
How quickly would I print (the world delighting)
A Grecian, Syrian, or *Assy*rian tale;
And sell you, mix'd with western Sentimentalism,
Some samples of the *finest Orientalism*.

(51)

Byron has already quickly printed, and had large readerships delight
in, his "samples of ... *Orientalism*" (for example, *The Giaour* and
'The Bride of Abydos' [1813]), yet it is as if those achievements are
of little account to him:

But I am but a nameless sort of person
(A broken Dandy lately on my travels)
And take for rhyme, to hook my rambling verse on,
The first that Walker's Lexicon unravels,
And when I can't find that, I put a worse on,
Not caring as I ought for critics' cavils ...

(52)

Compare the above description of the writer at work with, say,
Wordsworth's lifelong effort to convince the world that he never
actually *wrote* a word of poetry, but that it came to him on the breezes
as he walked over the moors and mountains of the Lake District.
Byron refused to put any of the usual disguises on the creative
impulses behind his poems. That meant that his creativity was allowed
to grow without constantly being pruned and qualified for tidy
inclusion in some impressive, but ultimately life-distorting scheme
of thought. If Byron lacked total control over his idiom, leading to
what Stabler has called "tonal instability" (*Byron, Poetics and History*,

75), then he shed the grace of his genius over the "failure", making his work unique:

> To turn, – and to return; – the Devil take it!
> This story slips for ever through my fingers,
> Because, just as the stanza likes to make it,
> It needs must be – and so it rather lingers;
> This form of verse began, I can't well break it,
> But must keep time and tune like public singers ...
>
> (63)

Lesser writers would try to mask that reality, and thus be forced at the outset to give up any attempt at being frank or naïve. They are unable to write what they think, because if they did, their work would look unsophisticated. So, they try to make readers believe that their thoughts have gone much deeper than is really the case. Their works draw attention because they say things in forced, unnatural ways, trembling between the two separate aims of communicating what they want to say and of concealing it. Their object is to dress up their ideas in order to give people the impression that there is very much more to them than for the moment meets the eye. Think of Aldous Huxley's (1894-1963) view of Wordsworth, who wrote such a vast amount of uninspiring poetry for the last forty years of his life:

> ... [Wordsworth] preferred to think his gifts away. He preferred, in the interests of preconceived religious theory, to ignore the disquieting strangeness of things, to interpret the impersonal diversity of Nature in terms of a divine, Anglican unity. He chose, in a word, to be a philosopher, comfortably at home with a manmade and, therefore, thoroughly comprehensible system, rather than a poet adventuring for adventure's sake through the mysterious world revealed by his direct and undistorted intuitions.
>
> (from 'Wordsworth in the Tropics', 1929)

At the age of 47, Wordsworth would publish the poem, 'Composed on an Evening of Extraordinary Beauty' (1817), which includes such lines as "Thine is the tranquil hour, purpureal eve", and prayers to God. Byron perceived in Wordsworth's, and other writers' strained, vague, prolix and cumbrous styles not just a waste of words, but also the trick of concealing poverty of thought under a stupefying farrago of never-ending chatter. The following, from *Detached Thoughts* illustrates Byron's concern:

66
One of my notions, different from those of my contemporaries,
is, that the present is not a high age of English Poetry: there
are *more* poets (soi-distant [self-serving]) than ever there were,
and proportionally *less* poetry.

Byron was a ferocious castigator of humbug, as the following attack on the poet William Sotheby ("*Botherby*" to Byron) demonstrates:

No solemn, antique gentleman of rhyme,
Who having angled all his life for Fame,
And getting but a nibble at a time,
Still fussily keeps fishing on, the same
Small "Triton of the minnows," the sublime
Of Mediocrity, the furious tame,
The Echo's echo, usher of the school
Of female wits, boy bards – in short, a fool!

(73)

A stalking oracle of awful phrase,
The approving "*Good!*" (by no means GOOD in law)
Humming like flies around the newest blaze,
The bluest of bluebottles you e'er saw,
Teasing with blame, excruciating with praise,
Gorging the little fame he gets all raw,
Translating tongues he knows not even by letter,
And sweating plays so middling, bad were better.

(74)

Away from England, Byron's poetry became more riotously clever. He was giving the English – "so suspicious", as Marsha Rowe has said, "of cleverness, fearing it to be superficial" (*So Very English*, 9) – even less reason to approve of him.

Hebrew Melodies and *Domestic Pieces*

Many people assume that at Byron's core there is merely the smashy pith of superficial talent rather than the solidity of real genius. His reputation as a lyric poet has been neglected because of his personality. We are over-supplied with information, and it runs away with the topic. Sometimes we are invited to admire his non-conformity, and sometimes we are encouraged to censure him as no more than a self-indulgent aristocratic pervert with no control over his lusts. The available candle-to-grave biographies, and the other accounts, tend to perpetuate the arbitrariness and circularity, and in that sense they are fictions revealing to us our fantasies about what we want Byron to be. It was like that during his day too. When Byron, and Percy and Mary Shelley, stayed in Switzerland in 1816, the local inhabitants suspected the strangers in their midst of orgiastic practices, and worse. "They looked upon me as a man-monster," complained Byron, who was, indeed, literally being looked upon. A local hotelier hired out telescopes so that British tourists could spy on the Byron household. Those tourists returned to Britain with colourful accounts of what they had 'seen'. In 1817, Southey commandeered the bandwagon, and announced that Byron and Shelley "had formed a league of incest". If there is anything that the 21st-century reader knows about Byron, it is that he was – in the words of Lady Caroline Lamb – "mad – bad – & dangerous to know". Yet his lyric poetry would make you ask: what was he really like?

His *Hebrew Melodies* are important pieces because of what, and whom, they relate to – the suffering of the Hebrews, "Israel's scattered race" that "cannot quit its place of birth" and "will not live" elsewhere:

> But we must wander witheringly,
> In other lands to die;
> And where our fathers' ashes be,
> Our own may never lie:
> Our temple hath not left a stone,
> And Mockery sits on Salem's throne.

> ('The Wild Gazelle')

In *Hebrew Melodies*, two different plights – the one of a famous, persecuted race and the other of a famous, persecuted poet – interanimate:

And where shall Israel lave her bleeding feet?
And when shall Zion's songs again seem sweet?
And Judah's melody once more rejoice
The hearts that leaped before its heavenly voice?

Tribes of the wandering foot and weary breast,
How shall ye flee away and be at rest!
The wild-dove hath her nest, the fox his cave,
Mankind their country – Israel but the grave!

('Oh! Weep For Those')

So it was not just in satire that Byron achieved greatness. His lyric poetry shows his other gift. 'She Walks in Beauty' opens with a phenomenal phrase: "She walks in Beauty, like the night". Quennell says that the line is "so magical that, by comparison, the rest of the poem appears to dwindle away into insignificance" (*Byron: The Years of Fame*, 200). True, the opening line of the poem has an exclamatory element, and from such an exclamation it is impossible for the poet to carry on at the same lyrical altitude. But there is also the necessity – which Quennell does not acknowledge – for the poet to *go into* the issue, and to explore the idea raised by the first line. In that way, Byron makes the poem complete:

And on that cheek, and o'er that brow,
So soft, so calm, yet eloquent,
The smiles that win, the tints that glow,
But tell of days in goodness spent ...

Byron knows about physiognomy, and knows that the prevailing facial expression of an individual (in this case, of "she" that "walks in beauty") is the result of a gradual process of innumerable, fleeting and characteristic contractions of the features. Yet Byron's knowledge does not become the snuffer component of a self-extinguishing poem. W.H. Auden (1907-73) often quenched his own flame almost as soon as he had kindled it. Auden could introduce a poem with a spark of verbal magic ("Lay your sleeping head, my love,/Human on my faithless arm", or "Out on the lawn I lie in bed"), only to end up ranting about the political ideas exchanged and received so routinely amongst the Oxbridge set of the 1930s:

And, gentle, do not care to know,
Where Poland draws her Eastern bow,
What violence is done;
Nor ask what doubtful acts allows
Our freedom in this English house,
Our picnics in the sun.

(From 'Out on the lawn I lie in bed')

Auden, like Byron existed in a homo-erotic society – where men
associated with men. But the similarity ends there: Byron also needed
women, especially those of capacious minds. His half-sister, Augusta,
had enough in common with him for them to be interested in each
other; and she was different enough from him for them to be attracted
to each other sexually:

I feel almost at times as I have felt
In happy childhood; trees, and flowers, and brooks,
Which do remember me of where I dwelt,
Ere my young mind was sacrificed to books,
Come as of yore upon me, and can melt
My heart with recognition of their looks;
And even at moments I could think I see
Some living thing to love – but none like thee.

('Epistle to Augusta', 7)

When Byron says to Augusta, "Oh that thou wert but with me!"
('Epistle to Augusta', 9), it is easy to think of Wordsworth's loving
address to his sister, Dorothy, in 'Lines composed a few miles above
Tintern Abbey' (1798):

For thou art with me here upon the banks
Of this fair river; thou my dearest Friend,
My dear, dear Friend; and in thy voice I catch
The language of my former heart, and read
My former pleasures in the shooting lights
Of thy wild eyes. Oh! yet a little while
May I behold in thee what I was once,
My dear, dear Sister!

Tender love, with the sexual component, is often behind the best
lyric poetry produced by Byron and Wordsworth. To imagine what it

would be like to receive the following from a lover now exiled in Italy is to form some sense of the pangs of star-crossed love:

1

Though the day of my Destiny's over,
And the star of my Fate hath declined,
Thy soft heart refused to discover
The faults which so many could find;
Though thy Soul with my grief was acquainted,
It shrunk not to share it with me,
And the Love which my Spirit hath painted
It never hath found but in *Thee*.

2

Then when Nature around me is smiling
The last smile which answers to mine,
I do not believe it beguiling
Because it reminds me of thine;
And when winds are at war with the ocean,
As the breasts I believed in with me,
If their billows excite an emotion,
It is that they bear me from *Thee*.

3

Though the rock of my last Hope is shiver'd,
And its fragments are sunk in the wave,
Though I feel that my soul is deliver'd
To Pain – it shall not be its slave.
There is many a pang to pursue me:
They may crush, but they shall not contemn –
They may torture, but shall not subdue me –
'Tis of *Thee* that I think – not of them.

4

Though human, thou didst not deceive me,
Though woman, thou didst not forsake,
Though loved, thou forborest to grieve me,
Though slander'd, thou never could'st shake, –
Though trusted, thou didst not betray me,
Though parted, it was not to fly,
Though watchful, 'twas not to defame me,
Nor, mute, that the world might belie.

5

Yet I blame not the World, nor despise it,
Nor the war of the many with one;
If my Soul was not fitted to prize it
'Twas folly not sooner to shun:
And if dearly that error hath cost me,
And more than I once could foresee,
I have found that, whatever it lost me,
It could not deprive me of *Thee*.

6

From the wreck of the past, which hath perish'd,
Thus much I at least may recall,
It hath taught me that what I most cherish'd
Deserved to be dearest of all:
In the Desert a fountain is springing,
In the wide waste there still is a tree,
And a bird in the solitude singing,
Which speaks to my spirit of *Thee*.

('Stanzas to Augusta', July 1816)

There is no hint of contrivance. The pain of separation, and yet the simultaneous pleasure of being able to think of one's lover so vividly that it can eclipse one's actual physical environment, is encapsulated with total confidence. When a poet has something to say, and says it, there is an instantly recognisable authenticity about the poem. The poem looks like an inevitable occurrence, like something we all knew, but had not yet happened in a poem.

In that respect, such poetry exists on its own terms, often at cross-purposes with the tools of literary criticism when the latter are applied. Applying the tools of literary criticism to the poem above, or the poem below, can be a little like dancing about architecture:

1

There's not a joy the world can give like that it takes away,
When the glow of early thought declines in Feeling's dull
    decay;
'Tis not on Youth's smooth cheek the blush alone, which
    fades so fast,
But the tender bloom of heart is gone, ere Youth itself be
    past.

Then the few whose spirits float above the wreck of
    happiness,
Are driven o'er the shoals of guilt or ocean of excess:
The magnet of their course is gone, or only points in vain
The shore to which their shiver'd sail shall never stretch
    again.

Then the mortal coldness of the soul like Death itself comes
    down;
It cannot feel for others' woes, it dare not dream its own;
That heavy chill has frozen o'er the fountain of our tears,
And tho' the eye may sparkle still, 'tis where the ice
    appears.

Tho' wit may flash from fluent lips, and mirth distract
    the breast,
Through midnight hours that yield no more their former
    hope of rest;
'Tis but as ivy-leaves around the ruin'd turret wreath,
All green and wildly fresh without but worn and grey
    beneath.

Oh could I feel as I have felt, – or be what I have been,
Or weep as I could once have wept, o'er many a vanished
    scene:
As springs in deserts found seem sweet, all brackish
    though they be,
So midst the wither'd waste of life, those tears would flow
    to me.

              ('Stanzas for Music', March 1815)

There is a consistency about the vast achievement of Byron's work.
He stood before the mystery of existence, knowing how to give
utterance to his non-knowledge of what existence is. He stood up to
what was wrong with people, including himself, and society, and
faced his world's faults in all their glaring enormity. He laughed
raucously at the corrective systems of thought on offer. He wove
lyrical spells, whose magic conveys that he loved tenderly, and

powerfully, and was, and will be, loved:

1

There be none of Beauty's daughters
With a magic like thee;
And like music on the waters
Is thy sweet voice to me:
When, as if its sound were causing
The charmèd Ocean's pausing,
The waves lie still and gleaming,
And the lulled winds seem dreaming;

2

And the Midnight Moon is weaving
Her bright chain o'er the deep;
Whose breast is gently heaving,
As an infant's asleep:
So the spirit bows before thee,
To listen and adore thee;
With a full but soft emotion,
Like the swell of Summer's ocean.

('Stanzas for Music', March 1816)

Don Juan

Langley-Moore has offered a plausible speculation as to *Don Juan*'s uncatchable oscillation between the sublime and the ridiculous:

> Byron was assiduous in the study of boxing, shooting and fencing, partly because he would naturally wish to master those physical accomplishments which, like swimming and horsemanship, could be practised despite his handicap, and partly because they were sporting activities of a man-about-town, and this was an aspect of his life that he had cultivated from early youth. It has seemed to some critics unworthy of a poet to care about the world of fashion, but his genius derived its sustenance from the variety of his experiences and all the contrasts they provided, which gives *Don Juan* its flashing interplay of poetical and mundane images.

(*Accounts Rendered*, 190)

And E.D. Hirsch has said:

> Of all Byron's poems *Don Juan* is the most Byronic not
> because it is more honest or less posing than the others (Byron
> never poses) but because it contains more of his astonishingly
> varied moods than any other: gloom, ecstasy, flippancy,
> indignation, pride, self-immersion, self-assertion, guilt,
> insouciance, sentimentality, nostalgia, optimism, pessimism.
>
> ('Byron and the Terrestrial Paradise')

Byron took the Don Juan idea and did a somersault with it. The joke
in *Don Juan* is that it is based on the myth of Don Giovanni, but
instead of the great seducer of the traditional tale, there is a hero
who in fact finds himself seduced by one woman after another. He is
much more of a passive character than the active rake that audiences
were used to. The interesting thing about *Don Juan* is that, in it,
Byron deconstructs the earlier poem, *Childe Harold*, the poem which
had made women throw themselves at him, because they confused
the writer with the hero he had created. The impact was made by the
image of the romantic hero who was mysterious, gloomy, brooding
and handsome. The gloomy reflecting hero suddenly becomes the
hero of *Don Juan* who has no kind of inner life or sense of memory
at all. Don Juan spends the first part of Canto II in a state of
melancholy at his departure from his native country, and weeping
over the love letter he has received from one of the women who has
seduced him:

18

"Farewell, my Spain! a long farewell!" he cried,
"Perhaps I may revisit thee no more,
But die, as many an exiled heart hath died,
Of its own thirst to see again thy shore:
Farewell, where Guadalquiver's waters glide!
Farewell, my mother! and, since all is o'er,
Farewell too, dearest Julia!" – (here he drew
Her letter out again, and read it through).

19

"And oh! if e'er I should forget, I swear –
But that's impossible, and cannot be –

Sooner shall this blue Ocean melt to air,
Sooner shall Earth resolve itself to sea,
Than I resign thine image, oh, my fair!
Or think of anything, excepting thee ...

A little later in the canto the letter is being torn up to be used as lots
to decide who is going to be the person that is eaten (the crew and
passengers are stranded upon the ocean, out of food, and about to
engage in cannibalism):

74

And none to be the sacrifice would choose;
At length the lots were torn up, and prepared,
But of materials that must shock the Muse –
Having no paper, for the want of better,
They took by force from Juan Julia's letter ...

The poem is a thoroughly debunking one, and it completely mystified
Byron's readers. This is one of the reasons why Hazlitt was unable
to stand Byron:

> A classical intoxication is followed by the splashing of soda-
> water, by frothy effusions of ordinary bile. After the lightning
> and the hurricane, we are introduced to the interior of the
> cabin and the contents of the wash-hand basins. The solemn
> hero of tragedy plays *Scrub* in the farce. This is "very tolerable
> and not to be endured." The Noble Lord is almost the only
> writer who has prostituted his talents in this way. He hallows
> in order to desecrate; takes a pleasure in defacing the images
> of beauty his hands have wrought; and raises our hopes and
> our beliefs in goodness only to dash them to the earth again,
> and break them in pieces the more effectively from the height
> they have fallen.

(*Spirit of the Age*)

Hazlitt saw Byron as not having high seriousness. Byron takes the
reader up, and then knocks him down – in the cannibal episode,
right down: Byron takes the reader from the first to the seventh circles
of hell:

75

The lots were made, and marked, and mixed, and handed
In silent horror, and their distribution
Lulled even the savage hunger which demanded,
Like the Promethean vulture , this pollution;
None in particular has sought or planned it,
'Twas Nature gnawed them to this resolution,
By which none were permitted to be neuter –
And the lot fell on Juan's luckless tutor.

76

He but requested to be bled to death:
The surgeon had his instruments, and bled
Pedrillo, and so gently ebbed his breath,
You hardly could perceive when he was dead.
He died as born, a Catholic in faith,
Like most in the belief in which they're bred,
And first a little crucifix he kissed,
And then held out his jugular and wrist.

77

The surgeon, as there was no other fee,
Had his first choice of morsels for his pains;
But being thirstiest at the moment, he
Preferred a draught from the fast-flowing veins:
Part was divided, part thrown in the sea,
And such things as the entrails and the brains
Regaled two sharks, who followed o'er the billow –
The sailors ate the rest of poor Pedrillo.

The above passage does not merely illustrate the writer's
desolating fascination with morbid detail. Byron the satirist had the
ability to capture the reality of being a modern human being, and he
often captured it with the ferocity of a collector driving a pin through
a social butterfly. There are still plenty of poets today working their
way across territory covered by Byron:

And all the little monsters said in a chorus:
You must kiss us.
What! You who are evil,
Ugly and uncivil.
You who are cruel,

Afraid and needy,
Uncouth and seedy.

Yes, moody and greedy.
Yes, you must bless us.

But the evil you do,
The endless ado.
Why bless you?
You are composed of such shameful stuff.
Because, said the monsters, beginning to laugh,
Because, they said, cheering up.
You might as well. You are part of us.

(Suniti Namjoshi, from 'The Ubiquitous Lout' in
St. Suniti and the Dragon [1994])

Hazlitt was unable to see that although the character of Don Juan is central, the bigger character was Byron, avoiding the easy option of playing the moralist, and instead showing readers in Regency England their secret selves' ferocious appetites. Earlier in the poem, Byron shows the surface stillness of Julia's temperament beginning to register the first tremors of desires gathering below:

Juan she saw, and, as a pretty child,
Caressed him often – such a thing might be
Quite innocently done, and harmless styled,
When she had twenty years, and thirteen he;
But I am not so sure I should have smiled
When he was sixteen, Julia twenty-three;
These few short years make wondrous alterations,
Particularly amongst sunburnt nations.

(I, 69)

Whate'er the cause might be, they had become
Changed; for the dame grew distant, the youth shy,
Their looks cast down, their greetings almost dumb,
And much embarrassment in either eye;
There surely will be little doubt with some
That Donna Julia knew the reason why,
But as for Juan, he had no more notion
Than he who never saw the sea, of Ocean.

(I, 70)

Byron traces very closely Donna Julia's silent explosion of inner lust. The passage is particularly subversive. It is one thing for a lady to look demure and practice piety, but it is another for her to contain her own unstoppable passions:

> Yet Julia's very coldness still was kind,
> And tremulously gentle her small hand
> Withdrew itself from his, but left behind
> A little pressure, thrilling, and so bland
> And slight, so very slight, that to the mind
> 'Twas but a doubt ...
>
> (I, 71)

> And if she met him, though she smiled no more,
> She looked a sadness sweeter than her smile,
> As if her heart had deeper thoughts in store
> She must not own, but cherished more the while,
> For that compression in its burning core;
> Even Innocence itself has many a wile,
> And will not dare to trust itself with truth,
> And Love is taught hypocrisy from youth.
>
> (I, 72)

The above stanza encapsulates the mechanism by which the respectable individual maintains her respectability, even when rattled by feelings that she simultaneously wants and does not want to have. Byron remains focused on this concept, and does not interrupt himself with the usual digression:

> But Passion most dissembles, yet betrays
> Even by its darkness; as the blackest sky
> Foretells the heaviest tempest, it displays
> Its workings through the vainly guarded eye,
> And in whatever aspect it arrays
> Itself, 't is still the same hypocrisy;
> Coldness or Anger, even Disdain or Hate,
> Are masks it often wears, and still too late.
>
> (I, 73)

His focus still uninterrupted, Byron ratchets up the sense of Julia's sexual tension. One realises the reason for the sustained focus: the

stanzas are gathering like a thunderhead of radical judgment over
the concept of monogamy:

> Then there were sighs, the deeper for suppression,
> And stolen glances, sweeter for the theft,
> And burning blushes, though for no transgression
> Tremblings when met, and restlessness when left;
> All these are little preludes to possession,
> Of which young Passion cannot be bereft ...
>
> (I, 74)

Becoming really strident now, Byron demonstrates that human desires
will flow despite the traditions built by humans to dam them:

> Poor Julia's heart was in an awkward state;
> She felt it going, and resolved to make
> The noblest efforts for herself and mate,
> For Honour's, Pride's, Religion's, Virtue's sake;
> Her resolutions were most truly great,
> And almost might have made a Tarquin quake;
> She pray'd the Virgin Mary for her grace,
> As being the best judge of a lady's case.
>
> (I, 75)

> She vowed she never would see Juan more,
> And next day paid a visit to his mother,
> And look'd extremely at the opening door,
> Which, by the Virgin's grace, let in another;
> Grateful she was, and yet a little sore –
> Again it opens, it can be no other,
> 'Tis surely Juan now – No! I'm afraid
> That night the Virgin was no further pray'd.
>
> (I, 76)

Byron has brought Julia to look over the moral precipice:

> She now determined that a virtuous woman
> Should rather face and overcome temptation,
> That flight was base and dastardly, and no man
> Should ever give her heart the least sensation;
> That is to say, a thought beyond the common
> Preference, that we must feel upon occasion,

For people who are pleasanter than others,
But then they only seem so many brothers.

(I, 77)

When Julia and Juan next meet, Byron again sustains his focus on Julia's inner struggle, and the precariously thin line that can divide 'Platonic' and sexual enthusiasm:

Julia had honour, virtue, truth, and love,
For Don Alfonso; and she inly swore,
By all the vows below to Powers above,
She never would disgrace the ring she wore,
Nor leave a wish which wisdom might reprove;
And while she ponder'd this, besides much more,
One hand on Juan's carelessly was thrown,
Quite by mistake – she thought it was her own;

(I, 109)

Unconsciously she lean'd upon the other,
Which play'd within the tangles of her hair;
And to contend with thoughts she could not smother,
She seem'd by the distraction of her air ...

(I, 110)

The hand which still held Juan's, by degrees
Gently, but palpably confirm'd its grasp,
As if it said, "Detain me, if you please";
Yet there's no doubt she only meant to clasp
His fingers with a pure Platonic squeeze ...

(I, 111)

His sense of humour continually intact, Byron plays Sophocles' Oedipus who, seeking enlightenment concerning a terrible truth, pursues his indefatigable enquiry, even when he divines that something appalling awaits him in the answer. But the poet carries in him too, like most of us, the Jocasta who begs Oedipus for God's sake not to enquire further:

... she must have thought there was no harm,
Or else 'twere easy to withdraw her waist;
But then the situation had its charm,

And then – God knows what next – I can't go on;
I'm almost sorry that I e'er begun.

(I, 115)

Byron inhabits a twilight region between comedy and high seriousness, which, because it cannot be cleanly identified as one or the other, has not had the attention it deserves:

> Oh Plato! Plato! you have paved the way,
> With your confounded fantasies, to more
> Immoral conduct by the fancied sway
> Your system feigns o'er the controlless core
> Of human hearts ...

(I, 116)

Byron's kick against Plato ("You're a bore"), is not entirely irresponsible – the plosive occurs like a relief at the end of an episode during which the narrator has maintained some level of impartiality.

Byron's challenging of received wisdom makes his work important today. People still believe things – not to mention die, kill, starve, marry, work for them – that are not necessarily true. The popular science writer, Richard Dawkins, has written a letter to his 10-year-old daughter, elucidating the problematic nature of belief:

> I simply want to ask where their [Christians', Jews', Muslims', Hindus', Sikhs'] beliefs came from. They came from tradition. Tradition means beliefs handed down from grandparent to parent to child, and so on. Or from books handed down through the centuries. Traditional beliefs often start from almost nothing; perhaps somebody just makes them up originally, like the stories about Thor and Zeus. But after they've been handed down over some centuries, the mere fact that they are so old makes them seem special. People believe things simply because people have believed the same thing over centuries. That's tradition.
>
> The trouble with tradition is that, no matter how long ago a story was made up, it is still exactly as true or untrue as the original story was. If you make up a story that isn't true, handing it down over any number of centuries doesn't make it any truer!

(A Devil's Chaplain, 286)

Dawkins' often bitter criticism of mind-numbing belief systems has made him, like Byron, a controversial figure. Schopenhauer was another, who longed for the "*euthanasia* of religion". When challenged about the dangers of depriving people of the sense of rightness in taking comfort from a faith-based system of belief, Schopenhauer said: "To free a man from error is to give, not to take away. Knowledge that a thing is false is a truth." (*Religion: A Dialogue*.) Dawkins and Schopenhauer are not without their senses of humour, but, if one reads their works at length, there is no escaping the feeling that they, too, are in a sense, tablets of stone with alternative commandments. Byron is special because the texture of his imagination is plastic and fun to play with. No commandments have been chiselled there because all is constantly changing, and, in short, irregularly *alive*. Byron did not stop, having attacked "History, Tradition …/newspapers…" (I, 203), but worked on to reveal a reality wondrous beyond the imaginings of tradition:

> But now at thirty years my hair is grey –
> (I wonder what it will be like at forty?
> I thought of a peruke the other day –)
> My heart is not much greener; and, in short, I
> Have squandered my whole summer while 'twas May,
> And feel no more the spirit to retort; I
> Have spent my life, both interest and principal,
> And deem not, what I deemed – my soul invincible.
>
> (I, 213)

> No more – no more – Oh! never more on me
> The freshness of the heart can fall like dew,
> Which out of all the lovely things we see
> Extracts emotions beautiful and new,
> Hived in our bosoms like the bag o' the bee:
> Think'st thou the honey with these objects grew?
> Alas! 'twas not in them, but in thy power
> To double even the sweetness of a flower.
>
> (I, 214)

> No more – no more – Oh! never more, my heart,
> Canst thou be my sole world, my universe!

Once all in all, but now a thing apart,
Thou canst not be my blessing or my curse ...

(I, 215)

Even when Byron feels scorched by reality's aridity, he paradoxically
teems as a creative force:

What is the end of fame? 'tis but to fill
A certain portion of uncertain paper:
Some liken it to climbing up a hill,
Whose summit, like all hills, is lost in vapour;
For this men write, speak, preach, and heroes kill,
And bards burn what they call their "midnight taper,"
To have, when the original is dust,
A name, a wretched picture and worse bust.

(I, 218)

What are the hopes of man? Old Egypt's King
Cheops erected the first Pyramid
And largest, thinking it was just the thing
To keep his memory whole, and mummy hid;
But somebody or other rummaging,
Burglariously broke his coffin's lid:
Let not a monument give you or me hopes,
Since not a pinch of dust remains of Cheops.

(I, 219)

5

Overview

Byron was given a rough time, and it has to be said that it was mainly because of prudery. In *Recollections of Lord Byron and Some of his Contemporaries* (1828), Leigh Hunt attacked his old patron and benefactor so nastily that John Murray quickly set about negotiating with Tom Moore for the latter to write Byron's biography:

> In consequence of Hunt's infamous publication respecting Lord Byron, I have felt it a duty no longer to withhold the means which I think I possess of doing justice to Lord Byron's character... I am therefore anxious for an opportunity of seeing you immediately.
>
> (25 January 1828)

Byron's achievements make up a complex picture. He was a lyric poet in a way that Pope was not. At the same time, he had the wit, and the "impatience", as Fowles says, "with existence that urged him to write" of Dryden, and the straightforwardness of Wilmot.

Why were the critics so hostile? When Byron's body was returned from Greece – "the only place I ever was contented in" – to England, his reputation was so bad that he could not possibly have been buried in Westminster Abbey or St. Paul's Cathedral. The paper, *John Bull*, jeered that Byron had:

> quitted the world at the most unfortunate period of his career, and in the most unsatisfactory manner – in voluntary exile, where his mind, debased by evil associations and the malignant brooding over imaginary ills, has been devoted to the construction of elaborate lampoons.

Byron's body was returned to Nottinghamshire. At his funeral, on 12 July 1824, the multitude of spectators did not care about the achievement of *Don Juan*, the *Hebrew Melodies*, or the *Turkish Tales*. But they did care about tales of incest and sodomy.

At Byron's funeral (the first celebrity funeral), John Clare (1793-1864) is recorded as having said:

> the Reverend the Moral and fastid[i]ous may say what they please about Lord Byron[']s fame and damn it as they list ... [but] the common people felt his merits ...
>
> (John Clare, *Autobiographical Writings*,
> ed. E. Robinson, 147)

Some literary historians have made bold to suggest that Byron's poetry has great merit, but the condemnation of the moralists found an influential voice. In 1924, Bishop Herbert E. Ryle effectively stymied another attempt to get Byron a place in Poets' Corner in Westminster:

> Byron, partly by his own openly dissolute life and partly by the influence of licentious verse, earned a worldwide reputation for immorality among English-speaking people. A man who outraged the laws of our Divine Lord, and whose treatment of women violated the Christian principles of purity and honor, should not be commemorated in Westminster Abbey.

Ryle spoke on behalf of the established church, which would not change the decision, despite the publication in the *Times* of a letter, in defence of Byron, from a group of people including Thomas Hardy (1840-1928), Rudyard Kipling (1865-1936) and three former Prime Ministers (Asquith [1852-1928], Balfour [1848-1930] and Lloyd George [1863-1945]).

Byron's work is a fascinating blend of real feeling *and* real sharpness. S.T. Coleridge said:

> according to the noble wont of the English people, Byron's literary merits would seem continually to rise, while his personal errors, if not denied, or altogether forgotten, would

be little noticed, & would be treated with ever softening gentleness.

(Collected Letters of Coleridge,
ed. E.L. Griggs, vol. V, 207)

Byron was not sexually repressed. He was sexually troubled, and driven irresistibly from within to anatomise that trouble. He did not have the inner serenity to retire and cultivate his spirit in silence. The unwieldy swirl in him of dust and deity precluded the recollection of emotion in tranquillity – as it precludes such recollection in most human beings.

There are writers who systematise and preach their systems. When we read their works, and when we are greatly impressed, we sometimes try to live our lives by those writers' precepts. But we often find that, for us, there is something wooden and unworkable about living one's life in, say, a Wordsworthian way, or in a Shelleyan way. To live strictly in accordance with another's precepts is to continually remind oneself that one is not good enough as one is. To have to act better than one is, is like walking with a pebble in one's shoe in order to remember to play the part of someone with a limp – it is false and painful. We human beings absolutely must, from time to time, flex our minds out of the constraints foisted upon us by systematisers. That is what Byron did all the time. He became the quintessence of that part of us which would break all the rules uninhibitedly.

There are people who regularly fail to practice what they preach, or what they claim to practice. They have instead realised that the important thing for them is to be seen to practice what they preach, or what they claim to practice. They are called hypocrites. As the term hypocrite may be predicated of an abominable number of people, it might provide a clue as to why so many people have treated Byron so harshly. In his engaging book, *Intellectuals* (1988), which exposes the inconsistencies and hypocrisies of those who preach the higher good, Paul Johnson:

> detect[s today] a certain public scepticism when intellectuals stand up to preach to us, a growing tendency among ordinary people to dispute the right of academics, writers and philosophers, eminent though they be, to tell us how to behave

113

and conduct our affairs. The belief seems to be spreading that intellectuals are no wiser as mentors, or worthier as exemplars, than the witch doctors or priests of old ...

Byron was able to see what Johnson calls "The worst of all despotisms[,] the heartless tyranny of ideas":

> Oh! ye great authors luminous, voluminous!
> Yet twice ten hundred thousand daily scribes!
> Whose pamphlets, volumes, newspapers, illumine us!
> Whether you're paid by government in bribes,
> To prove the public debt is not consuming us –
> Or, roughly treading on the "courtier's kibes"
> With clownish heel, your popular circulation
> Feeds you by printing half the realm's starvation –
>
> (*Don Juan*, IX, 35)

Byron knew the truth, then, of what Johnson has so recently, and provocatively, formulated:

> For intellectuals, far from being highly individualistic and non-conformist people, follow certain regular patterns of behaviour. Taken as a group, they are often ultra-conformist within the circles formed by those whose approval they seek and value. That is what makes them, *en masse*, so dangerous, for it enables them to create climates of opinion and prevailing orthodoxies, which themselves often generate irrational and destructive courses of action. Above all, we must at all times remember what intellectuals habitually forget: that people matter more than concepts and must come first.
>
> (*Intellectuals*, 342)

Byron is such an exuberant expression of the impulse in us all towards *freedom*, that churchmen, critics, literary theorists, and other people with wooden agendas have not really been very passionate about informing readers of the extents of Byron's two geniuses – as a lyric poet:

> My soul is dark – Oh! quickly string
> The harp I yet can brook to hear;
> And let thy gentle fingers fling

Its melting murmurs o'er mine ear.
If in this heart a hope be dear,
That sound shall charm it forth again:
If in these eyes there lurk a tear
'Twill flow, and cease to burn my brain.

But bid the strain be wild and deep,
Nor let thy notes of joy be first:
I tell thee, minstrel, I must weep,
Or else this heavy heart will burst;
For it hath been by sorrow nursed,
And ached in sleepless silence long;
And now 'tis doomed to know the worst,
And breaks at once – or yield to song.
('My Soul is Dark', Hebrew Melodies)

– and as a satirist:

But let it go: – it will one day be found
With other relics of "a former World,"
When this World shall be *former*, underground,
Thrown topsy-turvy, twisted, crisped, and curled,
Baked, fried, or burnt, turned inside-out, or drowned,
Like all the worlds before, which have been hurled
First out of, and then back again to chaos –
The superstratum which will overlay us.
(Don Juan, IX, 37)

While the detractors, and the purveyors of faint praise, have been
busy reducing Byron to something they could understand, Byron's
work has joyfully persisted on its own terms. To read Byron's work
is to know that the verbal universe he created has its own patterns of
interconnectivity, its own laws, and its own life:

The mind can make
Substance, and people planets of its own
With beings brighter than have been, and give
A breath to forms which can outlive all flesh.
(*The Dream*, 1816)

Selected Bibliography

The Poetical Works of Lord Byron, edited, with a memoir, by Ernest Hartley Coleridge (John Murray, Albemarle Street, London, 1905).

Byron's Poetry, selected and edited by Frank D. McConnell (Norton, 1978).

Eighteenth Century Verse, edited by Roger Lonsdale (Oxford, 1984).

Marilyn Butler, *Romantics, Rebels & Reactionaries: English Literature and its Background 1760-1830* (Oxford, 1981).

Rupert Christiansen, *Romantic Affinities* (Vintage, 1994).

Anthony Fowles, *John Dryden: A Critical Study* (Greenwich Exchange, 2003).

Caroline Franklin, *Byron: A Literary Life* (Macmillan Press Ltd., 2000).

Phyllis Grosskurth, *Byron: The Flawed Angel* (Sceptre, 1997).

Fiona MacCarthy, *Byron: Life and Legend* (Faber, 2003).

Jerome J. McGann, *Fiery Dust: Byron's Poetic Development* (The University of Chicago Press, 1968).

Doris Langley Moore, *Lord Byron: Accounts Rendered* (John Murray, 1974).

Tom Paulin, *The Day-Star of Liberty: William Hazlitt's Radical Style* (Faber, 1998).

Alexander Pope, *Selected Poetry*, selected by Douglas Grant (Penguin, 1985).

Peter Quennell, *Byron: The Years of Fame* (Penguin, 1954).

Bertrand Russell, *History of Western Philosophy* (Routledge, 1995).

Jane Stabler, *Byron, Poetics and History* (Cambridge University Press, 2002).

Francis Thompson, *Shelley* (Burns and Oates, London, [N.D]).

GREENWICH EXCHANGE BOOKS

STUDENT GUIDE LITERARY SERIES

The Greenwich Exchange Student Guide Literary Series is a collection of critical essays of major or contemporary serious writers in English and selected European languages. The series is for the student, the teacher and 'common readers' and is an ideal resource for libraries. The *Times Educational Supplement* praised these books, saying, "The style of [this series] has a pressure of meaning behind it. Readers should learn from that … If art is about selection, perception and taste, then this is it."

(ISBN prefix 1-871551- applies)
All books are paperbacks unless otherwise stated

The series includes:
W.H. Auden by Stephen Wade (36-6)
Honoré de Balzac by Wendy Mercer (48-X)
William Blake by Peter Davies (27-7)
The Brontës by Peter Davies (24-2)
Robert Browning by John Lucas (59-5)
Lord Byron by Andrew Keanie (83-9)
Samuel Taylor Coleridge by Andrew Keanie (64-1)
Joseph Conrad by Martin Seymour-Smith (18-8)
William Cowper by Michael Thorn (25-0)
Charles Dickens by Robert Giddings (26-9)
Emily Dickinson by Marnie Pomeroy (68-4)
John Donne by Sean Haldane (23-4)
Ford Madox Ford by Anthony Fowles (63-3)
The Stagecraft of Brian Friel by David Grant (74-9)
Robert Frost by Warren Hope (70-6)
Thomas Hardy by Sean Haldane (33-1)
Seamus Heaney by Warren Hope (37-4)
Joseph Heller by Anthony Fowles (84-6)
Gerard Manley Hopkins by Sean Sheehan (77-3)
James Joyce by Michael Murphy (73-0)
Laughter in the Dark – The Plays of Joe Orton by Arthur Burke (56-0)
Philip Larkin by Warren Hope (35-8)
Poets of the First World War by John Greening (79-X)
Philip Roth by Paul McDonald (72-2)
Shakespeare's *Macbeth* by Matt Simpson (69-2)
Shakespeare's *Othello* by Matt Simpson (71-4)

Shakespeare's *The Tempest* by Matt Simpson (75-7)
Shakespeare's *Twelfth Night* by Matt Simpson (86-2)
Shakespeare's **Non-Dramatic Poetry** by Martin Seymour-Smith (22-6)
Shakespeare's **Sonnets** by Martin Seymour-Smith (38-2)
Shakespeare's *The Winter's Tale* by John Lucas (80-3)
Tobias Smollett by Robert Giddings (21-8)
Dylan Thomas by Peter Davies (78-1)
Alfred, Lord Tennyson by Michael Thorn (20-X)
William Wordsworth by Andrew Keanie (57-9)
W.B. Yeats by John Greening (34-X)

LITERATURE & BIOGRAPHY

Matthew Arnold and 'Thyrsis' *by Patrick Carill Connolly*
Matthew Arnold (1822-1888) was a leading poet, intellect and aesthete of the Victorian epoch. He is now best known for his strictures as a literary and cultural critic, and educationist. After a long period of neglect, his views have come in for a re-evaluation. Arnold's poetry remains less well known, yet his poems and his understanding of poetry, which defied the conventions of his time, were central to his achievement.
The author traces Arnold's intellectual and poetic development, showing how his poetry gathers its meanings from a lifetime's study of European literature and philosophy. Connolly's unique exegesis of 'Thyrsis' draws upon a wide-ranging analysis of the pastoral and its associated myths in both classical and native cultures. This study shows lucidly and in detail how Arnold encouraged the intense reflection of the mind on the subject placed before it, believing in " … the all importance of the choice of the subject, the necessity of accurate observation; and subordinate character of expression."
Patrick Carill Connolly gained his English degree at Reading University and taught English literature abroad for a number of years before returning to Britain. He is now a civil servant living in London.
2004 • 180 pages • ISBN 1-871551-61-7

The Author, the Book and the Reader *by Robert Giddings*
This collection of essays analyses the effects of changing technology and the attendant commercial pressures on literary styles and subject matter. Authors covered include Charles Dickens, Tobias Smollett, Mark Twain, Dr Johnson and John le Carré.
1991 • 220 pages • illustrated • ISBN 1-871551-01-3

Aleister Crowley and the Cult of Pan *by Paul Newman*

Few more nightmarish figures stalk English literature than Aleister Crowley (1875-1947), poet, magician, mountaineer and agent provocateur. In this groundbreaking study, Paul Newman dives into the occult mire of Crowley's works and fishes out gems and grotesqueries that are by turns ethereal, sublime, pornographic and horrifying. Like Oscar Wilde before him, Crowley stood in "symbolic relationship to his age" and to contemporaries like Rupert Brooke, G.K. Chesterton and the Portuguese modernist, Fernando Pessoa. An influential exponent of the cult of the Great God Pan, his essentially 'pagan' outlook was shared by major European writers as well as English novelists like E.M. Forster, D.H. Lawrence and Arthur Machen.

Paul Newman lives in Cornwall. Editor of the literary magazine *Abraxas*, he has written over ten books.

2004 • 222 pages • ISBN 1-871551-66-8

John Dryden *by Anthony Fowles*

Of all the poets of the Augustan age, John Dryden was the most worldly. Anthony Fowles traces Dryden's evolution from 'wordsmith' to major poet. This critical study shows a poet of vigour and technical panache whose art was forged in the heat and battle of a turbulent polemical and pamphleteering age. Although Dryden's status as a literary critic has long been established, Fowles draws attention to his neglected achievements as a translator of poetry. He deals also with the less well-known aspects of Dryden's work – his plays and occasional pieces.

Born in London and educated at the Universities of Oxford and Southern California, Anthony Fowles began his career in film-making before becoming an author of film and television scripts and more than twenty books. Readers will welcome the many contemporary references to novels and film with which Fowles illuminates the life and work of this decisively influential English poetic voice.

2003 • 292 pages • ISBN 1-871551-58-7

The Good That We Do *by John Lucas*

John Lucas' book blends fiction, biography and social history in order to tell the story of his grandfather, Horace Kelly. Headteacher of a succession of elementary schools in impoverished areas of London, 'Hod' Kelly was also a keen cricketer, a devotee of the music hall, and included among his friends the great trade union leader Ernest Bevin. In telling the story of his life, Lucas has provided a fascinating range of insights into the lives of ordinary Londoners from the First World War until the outbreak of the Second World War. Threaded throughout is an account of such people's hunger for education, and of the different ways government, church and educational officialdom ministered to that hunger. *The Good That We Do* is both a study of one man and of a period when England changed, drastically and forever.

John Lucas is Professor Emeritus of the Universities of Loughborough and Nottingham Trent. He is the author of numerous works of a critical and scholarly nature and has published seven collections of poetry.

2001 • 214 pages • ISBN 1-871551-54-4

In Pursuit of Lewis Carroll *by Raphael Shaberman*
Sherlock Holmes and the author uncover new evidence in their investigations into the mysterious life and writing of Lewis Carroll. They examine published works by Carroll that have been overlooked by previous commentators. A newly-discovered poem, almost certainly by Carroll, is published here.

Amongst many aspects of Carroll's highly complex personality, this book explores his relationship with his parents, numerous child friends, and the formidable Mrs Liddell, mother of the immortal Alice. Raphael Shaberman was a founder member of the Lewis Carroll Society and a teacher of autistic children.

1994 • 118 pages • illustrated • ISBN 1-871551-13-7

Liar! Liar!: Jack Kerouac – Novelist *by R.J. Ellis*
The fullest study of Jack Kerouac's fiction to date. It is the first book to devote an individual chapter to every one of his novels. *On the Road*, *Visions of Cody* and *The Subterraneans* are reread in-depth, in a new and exciting way. *Visions of Gerard* and *Doctor Sax* are also strikingly reinterpreted, as are other daringly innovative writings, like 'The Railroad Earth' and his "try at a spontaneous *Finnegans Wake*" – *Old Angel Midnight*. Neglected writings, such as *Tristessa* and *Big Sur*, are also analysed, alongside better-known novels such as *Dharma Bums* and *Desolation Angels*.

R.J. Ellis is Senior Lecturer in English at Nottingham Trent University.

1999 • 294 pages • ISBN 1-871551-53-6

Musical Offering *by Yolanthe Leigh*
In a series of vivid sketches, anecdotes and reflections, Yolanthe Leigh tells the story of her growing up in the Poland of the 1930s and the Second World War. These are poignant episodes of a child's first encounters with both the enchantments and the cruelties of the world; and from a later time, stark memories of the brutality of the Nazi invasion, and the hardships of student life in Warsaw under the Occupation. But most of all this is a record of inward development; passages of remarkable intensity and simplicity

121

describe the girl's response to religion, to music, and to her discovery of philosophy.

Yolanthe Leigh was formerly a Lecturer in Philosophy at Reading University.

2000 • 56 pages • ISBN: 1-871551-46-3

Norman Cameron *by Warren Hope*
Norman Cameron's poetry was admired by W.H. Auden, celebrated by Dylan Thomas and valued by Robert Graves. He was described by Martin Seymour-Smith as, "one of ... the most rewarding and pure poets of his generation ..." and is at last given a full-length biography. This eminently sociable man, who had periods of darkness and despair, wrote little poetry by comparison with others of his time, but it is always of a consistently high quality – imaginative and profound.

2000 • 220 pages • illustrated • ISBN 1-871551-05-6

POETRY

Adam's Thoughts in Winter *by Warren Hope*
Warren Hope's poems have appeared from time to time in a number of literary periodicals, pamphlets and anthologies on both sides of the Atlantic. They appeal to lovers of poetry everywhere. His poems are brief, clear, frequently lyrical, characterised by wit, but often distinguished by tenderness. The poems gathered in this first book-length collection counter the brutalising ethos of contemporary life, speaking of, and for, the virtues of modesty, honesty and gentleness in an individual, memorable way.

2000 • 46 pages • ISBN 1-871551-40-4

Baudelaire: Les Fleurs du Mal *Translated by F.W. Leakey*
Selected poems from *Les Fleurs du Mal* are translated with parallel French texts and are designed to be read with pleasure by readers who have no French as well as those who are practised in the French language.

F.W. Leakey was Professor of French in the University of London. As a scholar, critic and teacher he specialised in the work of Baudelaire for 50 years and published a number of books on the poet.

2001 • 152 pages • ISBN 1-871551-10-2

'The Last Blackbird' and other poems by Ralph Hodgson *edited and introduced by John Harding*
Ralph Hodgson (1871-1962) was a poet and illustrator whose most influential and enduring work appeared to great acclaim just prior to, and during, the First World War. His work is imbued with a spiritual passion for

the beauty of creation and the mystery of existence. This new selection brings together, for the first time in 40 years, some of the most beautiful and powerful 'hymns to life' in the English language.

John Harding lives in London. He is a freelance writer and teacher and is Ralph Hodgson's biographer.

2004 • 70 pages • ISBN 1-871551-81-1

Lines from the Stone Age *by Sean Haldane*
Reviewing Sean Haldane's 1992 volume *Desire in Belfast*, Robert Nye wrote in *The Times* that "Haldane can be sure of his place among the English poets." This place is not yet a conspicuous one, mainly because his early volumes appeared in Canada, and because he has earned his living by other means than literature. Despite this, his poems have always had their circle of readers. The 60 previously unpublished poems of *Lines from the Stone Age* – "lines of longing, terror, pride, lust and pain" – may widen this circle.

2000 • 52 pages • ISBN 1-871551-39-0

Martin Seymour-Smith – Collected Poems *edited by Peter Davies* (180pp)
To the general public Martin Seymour-Smith (1928-1998) is known as a distinguished literary biographer, notably of Robert Graves, Rudyard Kipling and Thomas Hardy. To such figures as John Dover Wilson, William Empson, Stephen Spender and Anthony Burgess, he was regarded as one of the most independently-minded scholars of his generation, through his pioneering critical edition of Shakespeare's *Sonnets*, and his magisterial *Guide to Modern World Literature*.

To his fellow poets, Graves, James Reeves, C.H. Sisson and Robert Nye – he was first and foremost a poet. As this collection demonstrates, at the centre of the poems is a passionate engagement with Man, his sexuality and his personal relationships.

2005 • 182 pages • ISBN 1-871551-47-1

Shakespeare's Sonnets *by Martin Seymour-Smith*
Martin Seymour-Smith's outstanding achievement lies in the field of literary biography and criticism. In 1963 he produced his comprehensive edition, in the old spelling, of *Shakespeare's Sonnets* (here revised and corrected by himself and Peter Davies in 1998). With its landmark introduction and its brilliant critical commentary on each sonnet, it was praised by William Empson and John Dover Wilson. Stephen Spender said of him "I greatly admire Martin Seymour-Smith for the independence of his views and the great interest of his mind"; and both Robert Graves and Anthony Burgess described him as the leading critic of his time. His exegesis of the *Sonnets* remains unsurpassed.

2001 • 194 pages • ISBN 1-871551-38-2

The Rain and the Glass *by Robert Nye*

When Robert Nye's first poems were published, G.S. Fraser declared in the *Times Literary Supplement*: "Here is a proper poet, though it is hard to see how the larger literary public (greedy for flattery of their own concerns) could be brought to recognize that. But other proper poets – how many of them are left? – will recognize one of themselves."

Since then Nye has become known to a large public for his novels, especially *Falstaff* (1976), winner of the Hawthornden Prize and The Guardian Fiction Prize, and *The Late Mr Shakespeare* (1998). But his true vocation has always been poetry, and it is as a poet that he is best known to his fellow poets. "Nye is the inheritor of a poetic tradition that runs from Donne and Ralegh to Edward Thomas and Robert Graves," wrote James Aitchison in 1990, while the critic Gabriel Josipovici has described him as "one of the most interesting poets writing today, with a voice unlike that of any of his contemporaries".

This book contains all the poems Nye has written since his *Collected Poems* of 1995, together with his own selection from that volume. An introduction, telling the story of his poetic beginnings, affirms Nye's unfashionable belief in inspiration, as well as defining that quality of unforced truth which distinguishes the best of his work: "I have spent my life trying to write poems, but the poems gathered here came mostly when I was not."

2005 • 132 pages • ISBN 1-871551-41-2

Wilderness *by Martin Seymour-Smith*

This is Martin Seymour-Smith's first publication of his poetry for more than twenty years. This collection of 36 poems is a fearless account of an inner life of love, frustration, guilt, laughter and the celebration of others. He is best known to the general public as the author of the controversial and bestselling *Hardy* (1994).

1994 • 52 pages • ISBN 1-871551-08-0

BUSINESS

English Language Skills *by Vera Hughes*

If you want to be sure, (as a student, or in your business or personal life), that your written English is correct, this book is for you. Vera Hughes' aim is to help you to remember the basic rules of spelling, grammar and punctuation. 'Noun', 'verb', 'subject', 'object' and 'adjective' are the only technical terms used. The book teaches the clear, accurate English required by the business and office world. It coaches acceptable current usage and makes the rules easier to remember.

Vera Hughes was a civil servant and is a trainer and author of training manuals.

2002 • 142 pages • ISBN 1-871551-60-9

The Essential Accounting Dictionary of Key Financial Terms

by Linda Hodgson

This is a key aide for students seeking examination success in Accounting A-Level and GNVQ Advanced Business. It results from work with teachers and students and addresses common difficulties. Straightforward, easy to read definitions of key financial terms – which form the basis of understanding and better performance at tests and examination. There is a multiple choice quiz to crosscheck how much the student knows.

Linda Jane Hodgson, graduate in History and Politics, is a former Tax Inspector and qualified teacher. Professionally, she also advised accounting firms on taxation. She now teaches business and finance at a London college.

1999 • 150 pages • ISBN 1-871551-50-1